12.95

USEFUL BASIC PROGRAMS FOR THE IBM PC

USEFUL BASIC PROGRAMS FOR THE IBM PC

□ □ □

STANLEY R. TROST

BERKELEY • PARIS • DÜSSELDORF

Cover design by Sato Yamamoto
Design by Ingrid Owen

Library of Congress Card Number: 83-60487
ISBN 0-89588-111-X
Printed in the United States of America
10 9 8 7 6 5 4 3 2 1

ACKNOWLEDGEMENTS

Many people contributed ideas and hard work to this book. Rudolph Langer suggested the book and pointed the way to a number of improvements. Barbara Gordon edited the manuscript, checked the programs, and made many important suggestions. Joel Kreisman did the technical editing and prepared the programs for production. Many other members of the Sybex staff were also part of the team that put this book together.

Stan Trost
March 1983

CONTENTS

PREFACE

Useful BASIC Programs for the IBM PC will help you discover the full power and flexibility of your IBM Personal Computer. This book contains more than 65 practical programs and subroutines that are fully tested and ready to run; they provide a wide variety of business, personal, and educational applications. You do not need to understand the BASIC programming language to use these programs; you just enter them into your computer and use them for your own applications.

These programs will help you make important financial decisions; for example, you can find the break-even point of a new business, calculate the monthly payment necessary to establish a college fund for your children, and find the future value of regular deposits in an individual retirement account (IRA). The record keeping programs allow you to create a mailing list, phone directory, and automobile log. Students and nonstudents alike will find the mathematics practice programs especially useful. These practice programs help sharpen arithmetic skills; they can also help students with homework assignments.

Useful BASIC Programs for the IBM PC contains a number of unique programs. The fraction practice programs, long multiplication drill, record keeping programs, and combined data analysis and graphing programs are seldom, if ever, found in a collection of programs.

The use of standard subroutines is also unique to this book. A primary goal of this book is to provide programs that are *short* and easy to enter in your computer. To achieve this goal, the programs were created using a standard set of programs as subroutines. These subroutines will save you a great deal of effort when you create your own programs.

This book does not teach BASIC language programming; however, use of the programs will help you understand BASIC in a painless, almost automatic way. As you become familiar with BASIC, you will be able to modify the programs in this book and create new programs.

Let's now review the contents of the book. Chapter 1 gives instructions for using the programs and reviews the interactive features built into them. You should read this chapter before you use the programs.

Chapter 2 is a set of programs for home and business finance. It includes programs that calculate the future value of a bank deposit, the future value of a series of payments (for example, the future value of deposits in an IRA), the interest rate earned on an investment, and the time required to double your money. These programs can help you make many important investment decisions.

Chapter 3 contains a collection of business programs. These programs compute depreciation, the break-even point for a new business, wages earned with overtime, and decision analysis. The business programs will be helpful to business people, employees, and consumers.

In Chapter 4 we present real estate application programs including mortgage payments, balloon payments, and rental property analysis. You will, for example, be able to find the interest you can save by increasing your monthly house payment. Investors, homeowners, and prospective homeowners will find these programs helpful.

Chapter 5 includes a set of data analysis programs that can be used to analyze both scientific and financial data. The programs can compute mean and standard deviation, various moving averages, and linear regression, and they can graph the results. These programs can be of use in analyzing and projecting stock market trends, among other things.

Chapter 6 contains a set of record keeping programs to keep personal and automobile records. With these programs you will be able to use your computer to keep mailing lists and phone directories as well as mileage records for your car. The programs can be modified easily for other applications.

Chapter 7 presents a number of useful arithmetic drills for

students of all grade levels and abilities. These drills include addition, subtraction, multiplication, and division, using whole numbers as well as fractions. These programs can help sharpen your math skills and even help with homework!

We also include three appendices with this book. Appendix A lists the standard subroutines that enable the programs within the chapters to be so short. Their functions are described in REM statements. These subroutines are in numerical order so that you can easily refer to them. Appendix B shows you how to use these subroutines to create your own programs. Descriptions and examples are provided.

Appendix C lists several routines that allow you to use the full capabilities of your IBM printer. You can use these programs to gain access to all of the different printing modes available (condensed, expanded, double-strike, and so on).

□1 INTRODUCTION

This chapter shows you how *Useful BASIC Programs for the IBM PC* can greatly increase your computer's effectiveness. You will learn how to enter and run programs, create a subroutine library, and build a library of related programs that can run from a menu. You will also learn what interactive program design means and how it is accomplished in these programs.

The programs in this book do not require knowledge of the BASIC programming language. They can simply be used as is to solve a wide variety of business, home, and education problems. However, if you wish to expand your programming knowledge, these programs will show you how to take full advantage of the powerful features of your computer.

HOW TO START

The programs in this book run with cassette BASIC or disk BASIC. (You will need a disk for the programs in Chapter 6.) Review your BASIC manual for detailed instructions on loading and running BASIC.

To start cassette BASIC, raise the power switch to turn on your computer. If your computer has disk drives, leave the drive doors open. Cassette BASIC will start after a short pause.

Before you start disk BASIC, you must first start DOS. This is done by placing a DOS diskette in the left-hand drive and turning on the power. After a short pause the screen displays

```
>A
```

Now type BASIC and press the enter key. (The enter key is the key just above the PrtSc key.) Disk BASIC will now start. You should now remove the DOS diskette from the disk drive and put it away.

You will need two formatted disks (formatting instructions are in the IBM "Guide to Operations") to save the programs you enter (one as a master disk and one as a backup). You should always make two copies of every program.

At this point you can enter any of the programs in this book. You enter a program by typing the lines in the program listings exactly as they appear in this book. After each line press the enter key. Let's enter the following program:

```
100 PRINT "HELLO"
110 END
```

Begin by striking the Caps Lock key on your keyboard. This makes all of your input appear in uppercase. Now type the first line (100 PRINT "HELLO"). Enter this line by striking the enter key. Complete the program entry by typing and entering the second line.

You will sometimes make mistakes in entering the programs. Short lines are easily corrected by retyping the entire line. The IBM BASIC manual explains other methods you can use to correct errors on longer lines.

To run this program, type RUN 100 and strike the enter key. Notice the display on your screen; your program has printed HELLO below the program you entered. We'll give you more information on entering, saving, and running the programs later in this chapter.

REMARK STATEMENTS

We use *remarks* to make the programs easier to understand. Remark statements begin with the symbol REM or an apostrophe ('). In Figure 1.1, remarks make a border at the top of the program and explain the action of line 130. With one exception, you don't have to type the remarks as you enter the programs. The exception is that you must type the word REM on the first line of the program. The first REM is necessary because of the design of our programs. Figure 1.2 shows the same program listing after you type the necessary lines.

```
100 REM --------------
101 N$="SAMPLE PROGRAM"
102 REM --------------
110 INPUT X
120 INPUT Y
130 PRINT X+Y          'PRINT THE SUM OF X AND Y
140 END
```

Figure 1.1: Program Listing Including Remarks

```
100 REM
101 N$="SAMPLE PROGRAM"
110 INPUT X
120 INPUT Y
130 PRINT X+Y
140 END
```

Figure 1.2: Program Listing with Remarks Condensed

BUILDING A SUBROUTINE LIBRARY

The programs in this book use a central subroutine library to simplify program entry and output formatting. A *subroutine* is simply a program that is used as part of another program. For example, one central subroutine handles data entry for many of our programs. These subroutines allow our programs to be short and therefore easy for you to enter.

Appendix A contains the program listings for the subroutines you will use in this book. Appendix B shows you how to use some of these subroutines to create your own programs.

The following list shows the subroutines you must enter for the different chapters in this book. You should enter and save the subroutines on disk or tape as you need them; thus you need enter each subroutine only once. The numbers in the list refer to the first line number of each subroutine.

Chapters 2–7	3400, 5000, 5400, 5800, 6200, 6600 7000, 7400, 7800
Chapter 6	3000, 3800, 4600

We will begin by building the subroutine library for Chapters 2 through 5. Turn to Appendix A, where you will find the listings for the standard subroutines. Because the subroutine at line 3000 isn't needed until Chapter 6, begin with line 3400. Type the instructions for this subroutine into your computer. (Remember that remarks are not entered except in the first line.) Your entry should match that shown in Figure 1.3.

```
3400 REM
3420 Q1$="WOULD YOU LIKE TO "
3430 Q3$="AGAIN Y OR N"
3440 GOSUB 5000
3450 GOSUB 7800
3460 RETURN
```

Figure 1.3: Program Listing: ANOTH Subroutine

Continue to enter the rest of the subroutines necessary for Chapters 2–5. After you enter the standard routines, save them on disk or tape. Follow the instructions in the IBM "Guide to Operations" to ready your disk or tape. Then type

SAVE"SUBLIB",A

The ,A saves the programs in ASCII format. This format is necessary so that the subroutines can be merged later with the application programs.

Your central subroutine library is now stored under the file name SUBLIB. You will merge SUBLIB with your application programs when you run the applications. You should add the remainder of the subroutines to SUBLIB when you enter the programs in Chapter 6.

ENTERING AND RUNNING THE PROGRAMS

You are now ready to enter a program. Type the program instructions as they are shown in the program listings. The programs in Chapters 2, 3, and 4 should be saved in one file for each chapter. (Use file names that are meaningful to you.) The programs can then be run by loading the file for the desired chapter, merging the subroutine library, and typing RUN and the first line number of the desired program. When you have typed in all the programs in a chapter, you can create a menu to run the programs in that chapter. A menu is a list of programs that you can use to select the program you want to run. Instructions for creating the menu are given in each chapter. The programs in each chapter begin with unique line numbers; this allows you to store the programs and menu for each chapter together in one file.

For example, Chapter 2 contains a number of programs that are useful when you make financial calculations. Type in the Future Value of a Deposit program and save it on disk or tape by typing

```
SAVE"FIN
```

When you need another financial program, load the first financial program you saved by typing

```
LOAD"FIN
```

Now you can type in the next financial program you need. Save both programs together by typing

```
SAVE"FIN
```

You can see how this method enables you to build a library of financial programs.

Now let's run the Future Value of a Deposit program. Begin by using the LOAD command to load your program from disk or tape. Now use the MERGE command to merge the central subroutine library. Finally, run the program by typing RUN and the first line number:

```
LOAD"FIN
MERGE"SUBLIB
RUN 190
```

When you have typed in all the programs in Chapter 2, type in and save the Financial Programs Menu. This will enable you to run any program in that chapter by selecting it from the menu—no more line numbers to remember. To activate the menu program you should replace the END command in the last line of each program with a RETURN command.

The programs in Chapters 5–7 are entered in a slightly different way. They begin rather than end with a menu program, so in these chapters you first enter the menu and then the application program you choose. The programs are run by selecting them from the menu. Because we place the menus at the beginning of each set of programs in these chapters, you don't have to bother with replacing any END statements in the programs.

INTERACTIVE FEATURES

The word *interactive* refers to the interaction between the computer, the programs, and the user. The goal of an interactive program is to make it easy for the user to interact with the computer.

We accomplish this goal in various ways. When possible, we answer questions with a single keystroke that doesn't require the enter key. For example, programs are selected from the menus with a single digit, and yes/no questions require simply a Y or an N. Another interactive feature we use is to place all questions at the bottom of the screen, so you can always look for them in the same place. We also use sound to alert you to possible errors in input, particularly to incorrect answers in the arithmetic drills.

SUMMARY

This chapter provides you with detailed instructions for creating and saving a subroutine library and for using the library with the rest of the programs in this book. This chapter also tells you how to create a library of related programs that can be run from a menu. Each time you need a new program, you add it to the programs you have already saved.

The use of the central subroutine library allows the programs in this book to be very short and easy to enter, and the interactive features built into the programs make them easy to use.

□□2

HOME AND BUSINESS FINANCE

This chapter contains ten programs useful for many home and business finance applications. For example, let's assume that you are going to deposit money in a bank account for a specific term. One bank pays 8% compounded monthly, and another bank pays 8¼% compounded quarterly. With these programs you can use your computer to find which bank account pays more interest.

You may also wish to contribute regularly to an individual retirement account (IRA). With one of the programs in this chapter you can compute how much money you will have in your IRA at the time you retire. Another program allows you to see if an amount in a savings account is enough for you to retire with.

The last program in this chapter shows you how to put all the other programs together to produce a menu-controlled financial package.

FUTURE VALUE OF A DEPOSIT

Description

Have you ever wondered how quickly a savings account will grow? Would you like to compare the effect of different interest rates and compounding periods?

You can use this program to compute the future value of a deposit. You must specify the amount of the deposit, the number of times per year interest is compounded, the annual interest rate, and the number of years the funds will earn interest. The program assumes a constant interest rate.

Example

Tom deposits $5,000 in a four-year savings account. The bank pays interest at the rate of 12% per annum, compounded quarterly. Tom wishes to know how much his savings will grow in four years. Figure 2.1 shows the results of the computation on the screen. Figure 2.2 is the program listing for the Future Value program.

□□□

```
FUTURE VALUE OF DEPOSIT

   INITIAL DEPOSIT ($)     5,000.00
   PERIODS PER YEAR            4.00
   ANNUAL INT RATE (%)        12.00
   NUMBER OF YEARS             4.00

FUTURE VALUE              $8,023.53









-------------------------------------
WOULD YOU LIKE TO
COMPUTE
AGAIN Y OR N ?
```

Figure 2.1: Screen Display: Future Value of a Deposit

```
280 REM ------------------------------
290 N$=   "FUTURE VALUE OF DEPOSIT"
300 REM ------------------------------
310 GOSUB 6200 : K=1                         'INITIALIZE
320 REM ASK FOR PARAMETERS
330 Q1$="ENTER DATA" : Q2$=""
340 Q3$="INITIAL DEPOSIT ($)"       :GOSUB 6600
350 Q3$="PERIODS PER YEAR"          :GOSUB 6600
360 Q3$="ANNUAL INT RATE (%)"       :GOSUB 6600
370 Q3$="NUMBER OF YEARS"           :GOSUB 6600
380 REM DO THE COMPUTATION
390 PRINT
400 PRINT "FUTURE VALUE"; TAB(22)
410 A=PAR(1)
420 FOR I=1 TO PAR(2)*PAR(4)
430   A=A+A*PAR(3)/100/PAR(2)
440 NEXT I
450 A=INT(A*100+.5)/100
460 PRINT USING "$$######,.##" ; A
470 Q2$="COMPUTE" : GOSUB 3400          'ASK FOR ANOTHER
480 IF YN$="N" THEN END ELSE GOTO 280
```

Figure 2.2: Program Listing: Future Value of a Deposit

FUTURE VALUE OF A SERIES OF DEPOSITS

Description

This program calculates the future value of a series of regular deposits. For example, you can determine the future value of an IRA if you make regular annual contributions. You specify the amount of the payment, the number of payments made per year, the annual interest rate your funds earn, and the number of years you will make the payments. The program assumes that the compounding period and number of payments per year are the same, and that the annual interest rate is constant.

Example

Ann plans to deposit $500 in a savings account every month. Interest is earned at 6% per annum and is compounded monthly. How much money will be in her account in four years? Figure 2.3 shows the screen display for this example. The program listing is in Figure 2.4.

□□□

```
FUTURE VALUE OF SERIES

   PAYMENT ($)                    500.00
   PAYMENTS PER YEAR               12.00
   ANNUAL INT RATE (%)              6.00
   NUMBER OF YEARS                  4.00

FUTURE VALUE                  $27,048.92




----------------------------------------
WOULD YOU LIKE TO
COMPUTE
AGAIN Y OR N ?
```

Figure 2.3: Screen Display: Future Value of a Series of Deposits

```
490 REM ------------------------------
500 N$=     "FUTURE VALUE OF SERIES"
510 REM ------------------------------
520 GOSUB 6200 : K=1                          'INITIALIZE
530 REM  ASK FOR PARAMETERS
540 Q1$="ENTER DATA" : Q2$=""
550 Q3$="PAYMENT ($)"             :GOSUB 6600
560 Q3$="PAYMENTS PER YEAR"       :GOSUB 6600
570 Q3$="ANNUAL INT RATE (%)"     :GOSUB 6600
580 Q3$="NUMBER OF YEARS"         :GOSUB 6600
590 REM COMPUTE RESULT
600 PRINT : PRINT "FUTURE VALUE"; TAB(22)
610 A=0
620 FOR I = 1 TO PAR(2)*PAR(4)
630    A=PAR(1)+A +A*PAR(3)/100/PAR(2)
640 NEXT I
650 A= INT(A*100+.5)/100
660 PRINT USING "$$######,.##"; A
670 Q2$="COMPUTE" : GOSUB 3400               'ASK FOR ANOTHER
680 IF YN$="N" THEN END ELSE 520
```

Figure 2.4: Program Listing: Future Value of a Series of Deposits

PRESENT VALUE OF AN AMOUNT

Description

Assume that Bob owes you $5,000 in three years. He offers to pay you $4,000 today, and you want to know whether to accept his offer. The Present Value program uses an interest rate you specify to find the present value of a future amount. You should accept Bob's offer if the present value is less than $4,000.

To use this program you supply the future value, the annual interest rate at which your funds earn money, the number of compounding periods per year, and the number of years in the future that the value of the amount is known.

Example

Bill has a note for which he will receive $10,000 five years from now. Bill normally earns 10% interest on his funds, with interest being compounded quarterly. Bill would like to know the present value of his note. Figure 2.5 shows the screen display for the Present Value program; Figure 2.6 lists the Present Value program.

□□□

```
PRESENT VALUE OF AMOUNT

   FUTURE VALUE ($)        10,000.00
   PERIODS PER YEAR             4.00
   ANNUAL INT RATE (%)         10.00
   NUMBER OF YEARS              5.00

PRESENT VALUE              $6,102.71











----------------------------------------
WOULD YOU LIKE TO
COMPUTE
AGAIN Y OR N ?
```

Figure 2.5: Screen Display: Present Value of an Amount

```
690 REM ------------------------------
700 N$=   "PRESENT VALUE OF AMOUNT"
710 REM ------------------------------
720 GOSUB 6200 : K=1                      'INITIALIZE
730 REM  ASK FOR PARAMETERS
740 Q1$="ENTER DATA" : Q2$=""
750 Q3$="FUTURE VALUE ($)"      :GOSUB 6600
760 Q3$="PERIODS PER YEAR"      :GOSUB 6600
770 Q3$="ANNUAL INT RATE (%)"   :GOSUB 6600
780 Q3$="NUMBER OF YEARS"       :GOSUB 6600
790 REM DO THE COMPUTATION
800 PRINT : PRINT "PRESENT VALUE";TAB(22)
810 A=PAR(1)/(1+PAR(3)/100/PAR(2))^(PAR(2)*PAR(4))
820 A=INT(A*100+.5)/100
830 PRINT USING "$$######,.##"; A
840 Q2$="COMPUTE" : GOSUB 3400          'ASK FOR ANOTHER
850 IF YN$="N" THEN END ELSE GOTO 690
```

Figure 2.6: Program Listing: Present Value of an Amount

PRESENT VALUE OF A SERIES OF PAYMENTS

Description

The previous example shows you how to find the present value of a future amount. With this program you can find the present value of a series of payments. For example, assume that Sally buys your car and pays you $50 a month for three years. After one year she offers you $900 in cash, and you want to know whether to accept her offer. You can use this program to find the answer to your question. You should accept if the present value is less than $900.

To use this program you specify the amount of the payment, the number of payments you receive per year, the number of years for which the payments will continue, and the annual interest rate at which your funds earn interest. We assume that the number of payments per year and the number of compounding periods are identical.

Example

Jackie receives $400 per month in payments. She can earn 10% interest on invested funds, and she wants to know the present value of the payments. The payments will continue for ten years. Figure 2.7 shows the screen display for this example, and Figure 2.8 is the complete program listing.

□□□

```
PRESENT VALUE OF SERIES

  PAYMENT ($)                    400.00
  PAYMENTS PER YEAR               12.00
  ANNUAL INT RATE (%)             10.00
  NUMBER OF YEARS                 10.00

PRESENT VALUE                $30,268.52









----------------------------------------
WOULD YOU LIKE TO
COMPUTE
AGAIN Y OR N ?
```

Figure 2.7: Screen Display: Present Value of a Series of Payments

```
860 REM ------------------------------
870 N$=    "PRESENT VALUE OF SERIES"
880 REM ------------------------------
890 GOSUB 6200 : K=1                   'INITIALIZE
900 REM  ASK FOR PARAMETERS
910 Q3$="PAYMENT ($)"            :GOSUB 6600
920 Q3$="PAYMENTS PER YEAR"      :GOSUB 6600
930 Q3$="ANNUAL INT RATE (%)"    :GOSUB 6600
940 Q3$="NUMBER OF YEARS"        :GOSUB 6600
950 REM DO THE COMPUTATION
960 PRINT : PRINT "PRESENT VALUE";TAB(22)
970 A=0
980 FOR I = 1 TO PAR(2)*PAR(4)
990   A=A+PAR(1)/((1+PAR(3)/100/PAR(2))^I)
1000 NEXT I
1010 A=INT(A*100+.5)/100
1020 PRINT USING "$$######,.##"; A
1030 Q2$="COMPUTE" : GOSUB 3400        'ASK FOR ANOTHER
1040 IF YN$="N" THEN END ELSE GOTO 860
```

Figure 2.8: Program Listing: Present Value of a Series of Payments

PAYMENT REQUIRED FOR FUTURE SUM

Description

This program allows you to determine the regular payment necessary to produce a required amount of money in the future. For example, you can use this program to calculate what regular payments will be necessary to take a special vacation, replace a piece of equipment, or save for a college education. You must specify the future sum, the number of payments per year, the annual interest rate at which your funds earn interest, and the number of years to the time you need the money. The program assumes that the number of payments and the compounding periods are identical.

Example

Bob plans to make monthly payments into a college fund for his daughter. He will make the payments for 18 years, and he estimates that he will need $40,000. He can earn 8.5% interest on his college savings account. We show the screen display for this example in Figure 2.9 and the program listing in Figure 2.10.

□□□

```
PAYMENT REQD FOR FUTURE SUM

  FUTURE VALUE ($)        40,000.00
  PAYMENTS PER YEAR           12.00
  ANNUAL INT RATE (%)          8.50
  NUMBER OF YEARS             18.00

PAYMENT                      $78.85





----------------------------------------
WOULD YOU LIKE TO
COMPUTE
AGAIN Y OR N ?
```

Figure 2.9: Screen Display: Payment Required for Future Sum

```
1050 REM ------------------------------
1060 N$= "PAYMENT REQD FOR FUTURE SUM"
1070 REM ------------------------------
1080 GOSUB 6200 : K=1                    'INITIALIZE
1090 REM  ASK FOR PARAMETERS
1100 Q1$="ENTER DATA"   :Q2$=""
1110 Q3$="FUTURE VALUE ($)"            :GOSUB 6600
1120 Q3$="PAYMENTS PER YEAR"           :GOSUB 6600
1130 Q3$="ANNUAL INT RATE (%)"         :GOSUB 6600
1140 Q3$="NUMBER OF YEARS"             :GOSUB 6600
1150 REM DO THE COMPUTATION
1160 PRINT : PRINT "PAYMENT";TAB(22)
1170 I=PAR(3)/100/PAR(2)
1180 Q=PAR(2)*PAR(4)
1190 A=PAR(1)*I/((1+I)^Q-1)
1200 A=INT(A*100+.5)/100
1210 PRINT USING "$$######,.##"; A
1220 Q2$="COMPUTE" : GOSUB 3400          'ASK FOR ANOTHER
1230 IF YN$="N" THEN END ELSE GOTO 1050
```

Figure 2.10: Program Listing: Payment Required for Future Sum

WITHDRAWAL OF FUNDS

Description

You can use this program to determine how long you can make withdrawals from a bank account before the account runs out of funds. You must specify the initial deposit, the number of withdrawals per year, the interest rate at which the remaining funds earn interest, and the amount of the withdrawal. Again, the program assumes that the number of withdrawals per year and the number of compounding periods are identical.

If the withdrawal amount is less than the interest earned, your bank account will grow rather than run out of funds. The program then displays the message BANK BALANCE IS GROWING. Don't be concerned if this program takes a long time to finish running; the program executes as many times as is necessary to find a zero bank balance.

Example

Jack and Jill Jones are ready to retire. They have $200,000 in their bank account, and the account earns 9% interest. Jack and Jill plan to live on $1,600 per month. How long will they be able to withdraw money? Figure 2.11 shows the screen display for this example; the program is listed in Figure 2.12.

```
1240 REM ------------------------------
1250 N$=      "WITHDRAWAL OF FUNDS"
1260 REM ------------------------------
1270 GOSUB 6200 : K=1                        'INITIALIZE
1280 REM   ASK FOR PARAMETERS
1290 Q1$="ENTER DATA"   :Q2$=""
1300 Q3$="INITIAL DEPOSIT ($)"      :GOSUB 6600
1310 Q3$="WITHDWLS PER YEAR"        :GOSUB 6600
```

Figure 2.12: Program Listing: Withdrawal of Funds (continues)

```
WITHDRAWAL OF FUNDS

  INITIAL DEPOSIT ($)   200,000.00
  WITHDWLS PER YEAR          12.00
  ANNUAL INT RATE (%)         9.00
  PAYMENT ($)             1,600.00

PAYMENTS                    371.00
YEARS OF PAYMENTS            30.92











---------------------------------------
WOULD YOU LIKE TO
COMPUTE
AGAIN Y OR N ?
```

Figure 2.11: Screen Display: Withdrawal of Funds

```
1320 Q3$="ANNUAL INT RATE (%)"      :GOSUB 6600
1330 Q3$="PAYMENT ($)"              :GOSUB 6600
1340 REM DO THE COMPUTATION
1350 PRINT : PRINT "PAYMENTS";TAB(25)
1360 A=PAR(1)  : N=1
1370 A=A+A*PAR(3)/100/PAR(2)-PAR(4)
1380 IF A < PAR(1) THEN 1400
1390 PRINT: PRINT "BANK BALANCE IS GROWING"
1395 SOUND 500,9 :GOTO 1460
1400 IF A < PAR(4) THEN 1430
1410 N=N+1
1420 GOTO 1370
1430 PRINT USING "######.##"; N
1440 PRINT "YEARS OF PAYMENTS";TAB(25)
1450 PRINT USING "######.##"; N/12
1460 Q2$="COMPUTE" : GOSUB 3400        'ASK FOR ANOTHER
1470 IF YN$="N" THEN END ELSE GOTO 1240
```

Figure 2.12: Program Listing: Withdrawal of Funds

INTEREST RATE EARNED

Description

The program in this example is useful when you want to determine the interest rate you earn when you know the beginning and ending value of your investment. For example, you can find the equivalent interest rate on the profit from a house sale. To use this program you specify the beginning and ending values of your funds, the number of compounding periods per year, and the number of years over which your funds have grown.

Example

Auntie Mame gave $5,000 to her broker to invest four years ago. She has just received $9,000 in return. She wishes to compute the equivalent interest rate she has earned, with interest compounded quarterly. Figures 2.13 and 2.14 are the screen display and program listing for this example.

□□□

```
INTEREST RATE EARNED

  AMOUNT INVESTED ($)        5,000.00
  AMOUNT RETURNED ($)        9,000.00
  PERIODS PER YEAR               4.00
  NUMBER OF YEARS                4.00

ANNUAL INT RATE (%)             14.97




------------------------------------------
WOULD YOU LIKE TO
COMPUTE
AGAIN Y OR N ?
```

Figure 2.13: Screen Display: Interest Rate Earned

```
1480 REM ------------------------------
1490 N$=     "INTEREST RATE EARNED"
1500 REM ------------------------------
1510 GOSUB 6200 : K=1                    'INITIALIZE
1520 REM  ASK FOR PARAMETERS
1530 Q1$="ENTER DATA"   :Q2$=""
1540 Q3$="AMOUNT INVESTED ($)"    :GOSUB 6600
1550 Q3$="AMOUNT RETURNED ($)"    :GOSUB 6600
1560 Q3$="PERIODS PER YEAR"       :GOSUB 6600
1570 Q3$="NUMBER OF YEARS"        :GOSUB 6600
1580 REM DO THE COMPUTATION
1590 PRINT : PRINT "ANNUAL INT RATE (%)";TAB(24)
1600 Q=PAR(3)*PAR(4)
1610 I=((PAR(2)/PAR(1))^(1/Q)-1)*100*PAR(3)
1620 I=INT(I*100+.5)/100
1630 PRINT USING "######,.##"; I
1640 Q2$="COMPUTE" : GOSUB 3400          'ASK FOR ANOTHER
1650 IF YN$="N" THEN END ELSE GOTO 1480
```

Figure 2.14: Program Listing: Interest Rate Earned

NET PRESENT VALUE, UNEVEN CASH FLOWS

Description

Net present value (NPV) analysis is used by financial analysts to determine whether an investment is worthwhile. For an interest rate you specify, a positive NPV indicates that the investment is desirable.

This program is useful when you wish to determine the present value of a series of cash flows. The cash flows need not be the same in every period. You use this program by entering the initial investment you make and the annual interest rate at which your funds earn interest. The program then prompts you for each cash flow. You enter these cash flows as positive or negative numbers, depending on whether you receive or distribute funds. You signal the end of cash flow entries by striking the enter key.

Example

Tina can buy a note for $5,000. She will receive annual payments of $500, $1,500, $1,500, $1,500, and $1,000. Tina would like her funds to earn 12% annual interest. What is the net present value of her investment? The display in Figure 2.15 is negative, indicating that she is not earning 12%; thus she should not buy the note. A complete program listing is shown in Figure 2.16.

```
1660 REM -----------------------------------
1670 N$= "NET PRESENT VALUE, UNEVEN CASH FLOWS"
1680 REM -----------------------------------
1690 DIM PV(100)
1700 GOSUB 6200 :K=1                    'INITIALIZE
1710 REM   ASK FOR PARAMETERS
1720 Q1$="ENTER DATA"    :Q2$=""
1730 Q3$="AMOUNT INVESTED ($)"         :GOSUB 6600
1740 Q3$="ANNUAL INT RATE (%)"         :GOSUB 6600
1750 Q1$="ENTER ANNUAL CASH FLOWS"
1760 Q2$="IN ORDER RECEIVED"
1770 Q3$="STRIKE RETURN WHEN DONE"
1780 GOSUB 5000                         'ASK QUESTIONS
1790 J=10
1800 FOR I=1 TO 100
```

Figure 2.16: Program Listing:
Net Present Value, Uneven Cash Flows (continues)

```
NET PRESENT VALUE, UNEVEN CASH FLOWS

  AMOUNT INVESTED ($)     5,000.00
  ANNUAL INT RATE (%)        12.00


NET PRESENT VALUE          -$769.41


CASH FLOW  1 ? 500
CASH FLOW  2 ? 1500
CASH FLOW  3 ? 1500
CASH FLOW  4 ? 1500
CASH FLOW  5 ? 1000
CASH FLOW  6 ?




---------------------------------------
WOULD YOU LIKE TO
COMPUTE
AGAIN Y OR N ?
```

Figure 2.15: Screen Display: Net Present Value, Uneven Cash Flows

```
1810    LOCATE  J,1
1820    PRINT "CASH FLOW "+STR$(I);"          ";
1830    LOCATE J,14
1840    INPUT PV(I)                  'GET DATA & STORE
1850    IF PV(I)=0 THEN 1890
1860    J=J+1
1870    IF J=16 THEN J=10            'RESET POINTER
1880 NEXT I
1890 NPV=-PAR(1)
1900 FOR I=1 TO 100
1910    NPV= NPV+PV(I)/(1+PAR(2)/100)^I
1920 NEXT I
1930 LOCATE 6,1
1940 PRINT : PRINT "NET PRESENT VALUE";TAB(22)
1950 A=INT(NPV*100+.5)/100
1960 PRINT USING "$$######,.##"; A
1970 FOR I= 1 TO 100
1980  PV(I)=0
1990 NEXT I
2000 Q2$="COMPUTE" : GOSUB 3400  'ASK FOR ANOTHER
2010 IF YN$="N" THEN END ELSE GOTO 1700
```

Figure 2.16: Program Listing: Net Present Value, Uneven Cash Flows

TIME TO DOUBLE

Description

This program computes the time it will take for the funds you invest to double. To use the program you enter the annual interest rate and number of compounding periods per year.

Example

Fred's bank compounds interest four times yearly and pays 12% interest per annum. How many years will it take Fred to double a $5,000 investment? We display the results of this program in Figure 2.17; a program listing is shown in Figure 2.18.

□□□

```
TIME TO DOUBLE

  PERIODS PER YEAR                 4.00
  ANNUAL INT RATE (%)             12.00

TIME TO DOUBLE (YRS)               5.86




--------------------------------------
WOULD YOU LIKE TO
COMPUTE
AGAIN Y OR N ?
```

Figure 2.17: Screen Display: Time to Double

```
2020 REM ------------------------------
2030 N$=       "TIME TO DOUBLE"
2040 REM ------------------------------
2050 GOSUB 6200 : K=1                     'INITIALIZE
2060 REM  ASK FOR PARAMETERS
2070 Q1$="ENTER DATA"  :Q2$=""
2080 Q3$="PERIODS PER YEAR"       :GOSUB 6600
2090 Q3$="ANNUAL INT RATE (%)"    :GOSUB 6600
2100 REM DO THE COMPUTATION
2110 PRINT : PRINT "TIME TO DOUBLE (YRS)";TAB(25)
2120 I=PAR(2)/100/PAR(1)
2130 Y=LOG(2)/(PAR(1)*LOG(1+I))
2140 Y=INT(Y*100+.5)/100
2150 PRINT USING "######.##"; Y
2160 Q2$="COMPUTE" : GOSUB 3400          'ASK FOR ANOTHER
2170 IF YN$="N" THEN END ELSE GOTO 2050
```

Figure 2.18: Program Listing: Time to Double

EQUIVALENT INTEREST RATE

Description

Many of the programs in this chapter assume that the number of compounding periods and the number of payments are identical. This program allows you to determine an equivalent interest rate when the two periods are not the same. To use the program, enter the annual interest rate, the number of compounding periods, and the number of payments you want to make per year (desired periods). The program then computes an equivalent interest rate that you can use.

Example

You make deposits monthly into an account, and you wish to determine the future value of the deposits. The interest on this account is 12% per annum, compounded quarterly. As shown in Figure 2.19, the equivalent interest rate is 11.88%. You should use this figure and then run the Future Value of a Series of Deposits program to compute your final answer. The program listing for this example is given in Figure 2.20.

□□□

```
EQUIVALENT INTEREST RATE

  ANNUAL INT RATE (%)        12.00
  AVAILABLE PERIODS           4.00
  DESIRED   PERIODS          12.00

EQUIV INT RATE               11.88




----------------------------------------
WOULD YOU LIKE TO
COMPUTE
AGAIN Y OR N ?
```

Figure 2.19: Screen Display: Equivalent Interest Rate

```
2180 REM ------------------------------
2190 N$=   "EQUIVALENT INTEREST RATE"
2200 REM ------------------------------
2210 GOSUB 6200 : K=1                    'INITIALIZE
2220 REM  ASK FOR PARAMETERS
2230 Q1$="ENTER DATA"  :Q2$=""
2240 Q3$="ANNUAL INT RATE (%)"     :GOSUB 6600
2250 Q3$="AVAILABLE PERIODS  "     :GOSUB 6600
2260 Q3$="DESIRED   PERIODS  "     :GOSUB 6600
2270 I=PAR(1) : Q2=PAR(2) : Q1=PAR(3)
2280 IEQ=Q1*(1+I/100/Q2)^(Q2/Q1)-Q1
2290 PRINT : PRINT "EQUIV INT RATE";TAB(25)
2300 PRINT USING "######.##";IEQ*100
2310 Q2$="COMPUTE" : GOSUB 3400
2320 IF YN$="N" THEN END ELSE GOTO 2210
```

Figure 2.20: Program Listing: Equivalent Interest Rate

FINANCIAL PROGRAMS MENU

All of the programs in this chapter have been entered with distinct program line numbers. If you save all the programs together in one tape or diskette file, you can use the menu program we develop here to run any of these programs. The menu is set up so that you press a single key to select the program you want to run.

Remember, when these programs are used with the menu, you must replace the END instruction at the end of every program with a RETURN instruction. You should enter the menu program by first loading your financial programs, then keying in the menu program. Then save the programs and menu with the SAVE command. The menu is shown in Figure 2.21. Figure 2.22 shows the menu selection program.

After you have run the financial programs you need, you can return to BASIC to load another set of programs by pressing the control key and the break key together.

□□□

```
1 = FUTURE VALUE OF DEPOSIT
2 = FUTURE VALUE OF SERIES
3 = PRESENT VALUE OF AMOUNT
4 = PRESENT VALUE OF SERIES
5 = PAYMENT REQD FOR FUTURE SUM
6 = WITHDRAWAL OF FUNDS
7 = INTEREST RATE EARNED
8 = NET PRESENT VALUE, UNEVEN CASH FLOWS
9 = TIME TO DOUBLE
0 = EQUIVALENT INTEREST RATE



-----------------------------------------


CHOOSE PROGRAM :
```

Figure 2.21: Screen Display: Financial Programs Menu

```
100 REM ------------------------------
110 N$=       "FINANCIAL PROGRAMS"
120 REM ------------------------------
130 GOSUB 6200                             'INITIALIZE
140 REM SET UP MENU ARRAY
150 X$(1)="FUTURE VALUE OF DEPOSIT"
160 X$(2)="FUTURE VALUE OF SERIES
170 X$(3)="PRESENT VALUE OF AMOUNT"
180 X$(4)="PRESENT VALUE OF SERIES"
190 X$(5)="PAYMENT REQD FOR FUTURE SUM"
200 X$(6)="WITHDRAWAL OF FUNDS"
210 X$(7)="INTEREST RATE EARNED"
220 X$(8)="NET PRESENT VALUE, UNEVEN CASH FLOWS"
230 X$(9)="TIME TO DOUBLE"
240 X$(10)="EQUIVALENT INTEREST RATE"
250 N=10:  GOSUB 7000                      'DISPLAY MENU
259 REM SELECT PROGRAM
260 ON X GOSUB 280,490,690,860,1050,1240,1480,1660,2020,2180
270 GOTO 100
```

Figure 2.22: Program Listing: Financial Programs Menu

□□□ 3

USEFUL BUSINESS PROGRAMS

This chapter presents ten helpful business programs. These programs enable you to prepare depreciation schedules, find the economic ordering quantity, and solve many other business problems.

For example, you may be starting a business or running a charity event; the Break-Even Point program will calculate how many items or tickets you must sell to produce a profit. Whether you are a salesperson or employ a salesperson, the Salesperson's Commission program allows you to find the commission due for a given sales volume. The Wages with Overtime program makes it simple to calculate the salary due when overtime is worked. This program adds base pay and overtime pay to find the total salary due. We also provide an executive decision making program, which can be used when all else fails.

Remember to save these programs as you enter them and to merge the central subroutines prior to running the programs.

STRAIGHT-LINE DEPRECIATION

Description

This program computes a yearly depreciation schedule based on the straight-line method. To depreciate an asset, you specify the present book value, the estimated salvage value, and the life of the asset in years. If your asset has a life longer than twelve years, the program displays the schedule for the first twelve years and then pauses. When you are ready to review years 13–24, you simply press any key, and the schedule for those years is displayed.

Example

Let's set up a depreciation schedule for an office copier. We presently value the copier at $5,000. We expect to use the copier for six years and then sell it for $1,000. Figure 3.1 shows the screen display of the depreciation schedule. Figure 3.2 is a listing of the depreciation program.

□□□

```
STRAIGHT-LINE DEPRECIATION

  PRES. BOOK VALUE ($)    5,000.00
  SALVAGE VALUE ($)       1,000.00
  LIFE (YRS)                  6.00

YEAR      DEPR($)    VALUE($)
 1         666.67    4,333.33
 2         666.67    3,666.67
 3         666.67    3,000.00
 4         666.67    2,333.33
 5         666.67    1,666.67
 6         666.67    1,000.00




----------------------------------------
WOULD YOU LIKE TO
COMPUTE
AGAIN Y OR N ?
```

Figure 3.1: Screen Display: Straight-Line Depreciation

```
280 REM ----------------------------------
290 N$=    "STRAIGHT-LINE DEPRECIATION"
300 REM ----------------------------------
310 GOSUB 6200 : K=1
320 REM GET INPUT PARAMETERS
330 Q1$="ENTER DATA" : Q2$=""
340 Q3$="PRES. BOOK VALUE ($)"     : GOSUB 6600
350 Q3$="SALVAGE VALUE ($)"        : GOSUB 6600
360 Q3$="LIFE (YRS) "              : GOSUB 6600
370 REM PRINT DEPR SCHEDULE
380 D=(PAR(1)-PAR(2))/PAR(3)
390 PRINT
400 PRINT"YEAR     DEPR($)   VALUE($)"
410 FOR A= 1 TO PAR(3)
420   PRINT A; TAB(6);
430   PRINT USING "#######,.##";D,PAR(1)-D*A
440   IF A <> 12 THEN 470
450   GOSUB 7400                        'WAIT FOR KEY
460   LOCATE 8,1                        'RESET POINTER
470 NEXT A
480 Q2$="COMPUTE"  : GOSUB 3400         'ASK FOR ANOTHER
490 IF YN$="N" THEN END ELSE GOTO 280
```

Figure 3.2: Program Listing: Straight-Line Depreciation

DECLINING-BALANCE DEPRECIATION

Description

This program makes it easy to calculate depreciation schedules based on the declining-balance method, which is an accelerated method of depreciation. Accelerated depreciation methods are often used to provide more favorable tax treatment than the straight-line method provides. The declining-balance method multiplies the remaining book value of an asset by an acceleration factor and then divides by the life of the asset in years. You must specify the initial book value of the asset, its useful life, and the acceleration factor. Typical acceleration factors are 150%, 175%, and 200%; the salvage value is not used.

Example

Let's now depreciate the office copier in the previous example by the declining-balance method. In this example we use an acceleration factor of 150%. The depreciation schedule appears in Figure 3.3 and the program listing in Figure 3.4.

```
500 REM ---------------------------------------
510 N$=      "DECLINING-BALANCE DEPRECIATION"
520 REM ---------------------------------------
530 GOSUB 6200 : K=1
540 REM GET INPUT PARAMETERS
550 Q1$="ENTER DATA" : Q2$=""
560 Q3$="PRES. BOOK VALUE ($)"       : GOSUB 6600
570 Q3$="LIFE (YRS) "                : GOSUB 6600
580 Q3$="% ACCEL DEPRECIATION"       : GOSUB 6600
```

Figure 3.4: Program Listing: Declining-Balance Depreciation (continues)

```
DECLINING-BALANCE DEPRECIATION

  PRES. BOOK VALUE ($)    5,000.00
  LIFE (YRS)                  6.00
  % ACCEL DEPRECIATION      150.00

YEAR       DEPR($)    VALUE($)
 1        1,250.00    3,750.00
 2          937.50    2,812.50
 3          703.13    2,109.38
 4          527.34    1,582.03
 5          395.51    1,186.52
 6          296.63      889.89




----------------------------------------
WOULD YOU LIKE TO
COMPUTE
AGAIN Y OR N ?
```

Figure 3.3: Screen Display: Declining-Balance Depreciation

```
590 REM PRINT DEPR SCHEDULE
600 RV=PAR(1)
610 PRINT
620 PRINT"YEAR     DEPR($)    VALUE($)"
630 FOR A= 1 TO PAR(2)
640   PRINT A; TAB(6);
650   D=RV*PAR(3)/100/PAR(2)
660   PRINT USING "#######,.##";D,RV-D
670   RV=RV-D
680   IF A <> 12 THEN 710
690   GOSUB 7400                     'WAIT
700   LOCATE 8,1
710 NEXT A
720 Q2$="COMPUTE"  : GOSUB 3400      'ASK FOR ANOTHER
730 IF YN$="N" THEN END ELSE GOTO 500
```

Figure 3.4: Program Listing: Declining-Balance Depreciation

SUM-OF-YEARS'-DIGITS DEPRECIATION

Description

We now show a second method of accelerated depreciation, the sum of the years' digits. This depreciation method multiplies the remaining book value by the ratio of the number of remaining years to the sum of the years of life. If the life of the asset is five years, the sum of the years of life is

$$5 + 4 + 3 + 2 + 1 = 15$$

You again specify the present book value, salvage value, and life of the asset. Your computer simplifies the otherwise tedious calculation.

Example

Let us produce a sum-of-the-years'-digits depreciation schedule for the office copier in the prior examples. The schedule is shown in Figure 3.5; the program listing appears in Figure 3.6.

```
740 REM ----------------------------------------
750 N$=      "SUM-OF-YEARS'-DIGITS DEPRECIATION"
760 REM ----------------------------------------
770 GOSUB 6200 : K=1
780 REM GET INPUT PARAMETERS
790 Q1$="ENTER DATA" : Q2$=""
800 Q3$="PRES. BOOK VALUE ($)"       : GOSUB 6600
810 Q3$="SALVAGE VALUE ($)"          : GOSUB 6600
```

Figure 3.6: Program Listing: Sum-of-Years'-Digits Depreciation (continues)

```
SUM-OF-YEARS'-DIGITS DEPRECIATION

  PRES. BOOK VALUE ($)    5,000.00
  SALVAGE VALUE ($)       1,000.00
  LIFE (YRS)                  6.00

YEAR      DEPR($)    VALUE($)
 1       1,142.86    3,857.14
 2         952.38    2,904.76
 3         761.90    2,142.86
 4         571.43    1,571.43
 5         380.95    1,190.48
 6         190.48    1,000.00




----------------------------------------
WOULD YOU LIKE TO
COMPUTE
AGAIN Y OR N ?
```

Figure 3.5: Screen Display: Sum-of-Years'-Digits Depreciation

```
820 Q3$="LIFE (YRS) "                : GOSUB 6600
830 REM PRINT DEPR SCHEDULE
840 D=PAR(1)-PAR(2)
850 RV=PAR(1)
860 PRINT
870 PRINT"YEAR     DEPR($)    VALUE($)"
880 FOR A= 1 TO PAR(3)
890   D1=D*(PAR(3)+1-A)/(PAR(3)*(PAR(3)+1)/2)
900   PRINT A; TAB(6);
910   PRINT USING "#######,.##";D1,RV-D1
920   RV=RV-D1
930   IF A <> 12 THEN 960
940   GOSUB 7400
950   LOCATE 8,1
960 NEXT A
970 Q2$="COMPUTE"  : GOSUB 3400       'ASK FOR ANOTHER
980 IF YN$="N" THEN END ELSE GOTO 740
```

Figure 3.6: Program Listing: Sum-of-Years'-Digits Depreciation

BREAK-EVEN POINT

Description

This program allows you to find the number of items you must sell for a business or product line to break even. To use this program you must specify the fixed costs of the business (overhead), the cost per unit to manufacture or buy your product, and the sales price per unit.

Example

Harry buys novelty items for $3.00 each and plans to sell them for $6.00 each through mail order. If Harry plans to spend $1,500 for advertising, how many units must he sell to break even? The screen display for this example is shown in Figure 3.7; the program listing appears in Figure 3.8.

□□□

```
BREAK-EVEN POINT

   FIXED COSTS ($)           1,500.00
   COST PER UNIT ($)             3.00
   SALES PRICE ($)               6.00

BREAK-EVEN POINT ->       500 UNITS




----------------------------------------
WOULD YOU LIKE TO
COMPUTE
AGAIN Y OR N ?
```

Figure 3.7: Screen Display: Break-Even Point

```
990 REM ------------------------------
1000 N$=      "BREAK-EVEN POINT"
1010 REM ------------------------------
1020 GOSUB 6200 : K=1
1030 REM GET INPUT PARAMETERS
1040 Q1$="ENTER DATA" : Q2$=""
1050 Q3$="FIXED COSTS ($)"    : GOSUB 6600
1060 Q3$="COST PER UNIT ($)" : GOSUB 6600
1070 Q3$="SALES PRICE ($)"    : GOSUB 6600
1080 PRINT
1090 PRINT "BREAK-EVEN POINT ->  ";
1100 US=INT(PAR(1)/(PAR(3)-PAR(2))*100+.5)/100
1110 PRINT USING "#####,"; US; :PRINT " UNITS"
1120 Q2$="COMPUTE"  : GOSUB 3400       'ASK FOR ANOTHER
1130 IF YN$="N" THEN END ELSE GOTO 990
```

Figure 3.8: Program Listing: Break-Even Point

ECONOMIC ORDERING QUANTITY

Description

Operations researchers have developed a method to compute the most economic quantity of items for a manufacturer to order. This program does the computation for you. To use this program, specify the cost to place a purchase order, the number of units you use annually, and the annual carrying cost per unit. Carrying cost is defined as the interest rate your funds earn multiplied by the purchase price per item.

Example

Ray is the production manager for a small manufacturing company. He wants to calculate the economic ordering quantity for pumps that are used in the company's products. The company uses 15,000 pumps annually. The annual carrying cost of the pumps is $5 each, and a purchase order costs $75. What is the economic ordering quantity? Figure 3.9 shows the result of Ray's analysis. Figure 3.10 displays the program listing.

□□□

```
ECONOMIC ORDERING QUANTITY

  COST TO ORDER ($)             75.00
  ANNUAL UNITS USED         15,000.00
  UNIT CARRYING COST($)          5.00

    EOQ =     670 UNITS









----------------------------------------
WOULD YOU LIKE TO
COMPUTE
AGAIN Y OR N ?
```

Figure 3.9: Screen Display: Economic Ordering Quantity

```
1140 REM ------------------------------------
1150 N$=     "ECONOMIC ORDERING QUANTITY"
1160 REM ------------------------------------
1170 GOSUB 6200 : K=1
1180 REM GET INPUT PARAMETERS
1190 Q1$="ENTER DATA" : Q2$=""
1200 Q3$="COST TO ORDER ($)"       : GOSUB 6600
1210 Q3$="ANNUAL UNITS USED "      : GOSUB 6600
1220 Q3$="UNIT CARRYING COST($)"   : GOSUB 6600
1230 REM COMPUTE AND PRINT
1240 PRINT
1250 EOQ=INT(SQR(2*PAR(1)*PAR(2)/PAR(3)))
1260 PRINT "    EOQ = ";
1270 PRINT USING "#####,"; EOQ;
1280 PRINT " UNITS"
1290 Q2$="COMPUTE"  : GOSUB 3400      'ASK FOR ANOTHER
1300 IF YN$="N" THEN END ELSE GOTO 1140
```

Figure 3.10: Program Listing: Economic Ordering Quantity

SALES PRICE WITH DISCOUNT

Description

Here is a program that enables you to compute the total sales price, with tax, of an item that is selling at a discount. To use this program you specify the retail price, discount percentage, and sales tax rate.

Example

Betty wants to buy a television set that is being sold at a 15% discount. The retail price of the television set is $350 and the sales tax is 6.5%. How much will Betty have to pay? Figure 3.11 shows the screen display for this example. Figure 3.12 shows the listing for the Sales Price with Discount program.

```
1310 REM ------------------------------------
1320 N$=      "SALES PRICE WITH DISCOUNT"
1330 REM ------------------------------------
1340 GOSUB 6200 : K=1
1350 REM GET INPUT PARAMETERS
1360 Q1$="ENTER DATA" : Q2$=""
1370 Q3$="RETAIL PRICE ($)"   : GOSUB 6600
1380 Q3$="DISCOUNT (%)"       : GOSUB 6600
```

Figure 3.12: Program Listing: Sales Price with Discount (continues)

```
SALES PRICE WITH DISCOUNT

  RETAIL PRICE ($)          350.00
  DISCOUNT (%)               15.00
  SALES TAX (%)               6.50

  PRICE                    $350.00
  DISCOUNT                  $52.50
  TAX                       $19.34

TOTAL                      $316.84





----------------------------------------
WOULD YOU LIKE TO
COMPUTE
AGAIN Y OR N ?
```

Figure 3.11: Screen Display: Sales Price with Discount

```
1390 Q3$="SALES TAX (%)"      : GOSUB 6600
1400 REM COMPUTE AND PRINT
1410 PRINT
1420 PRINT "  PRICE";TAB(24);
1430 PRINT USING "$$####,.##";PAR(1)
1440 D=PAR(1)*PAR(2)/100
1450 PRINT "  DISCOUNT";TAB(24);
1460 PRINT USING "$$####,.##";D
1470 T=(PAR(1)-D)*PAR(3)/100
1480 PRINT "  TAX";TAB(24);
1490 PRINT USING "$$####,.##";T
1500 PRINT
1510 PRINT "TOTAL";TAB(24);
1520 PRINT USING "$$####,.##";PAR(1)-D+T
1530 Q2$="COMPUTE"  : GOSUB 3400      'ASK FOR ANOTHER
1540 IF YN$="N" THEN END ELSE GOTO 1310
```

Figure 3.12: Program Listing: Sales Price with Discount

WEIGHTED AVERAGE

Description

There are many times when you will need to compute the weighted average of a number of items. Weighted averages can be used to find the average cost of stocks when you buy shares of stock at different times and different values. Weighted averages are also one way of finding the value of a business's inventory when the same item is bought at different prices.

This program rapidly computes the weighted average of a series of quantities. You use the program by entering a unit value followed by the number of units for each item. You end the entry process by striking the enter key without entering data.

Example

Lloyd has been buying stock in a rapidly appreciating electronics company. He would like to calculate his average cost of shares; he has purchased four shares at $10 each, four shares at $40 each, and two shares at $60 each. Figures 3.13 and 3.14 show the result of the calculation and the program listing.

```
1550 REM ------------------------------
1560 N$=      "WEIGHTED AVERAGE"
1570 REM ------------------------------
1580 DIM D(100,1)
1590 GOSUB 6200 : K=1
1600 REM GET INPUT PARAMETERS
1610 PRINT "ENTER DATA, RETURN WHEN DONE"
1620 PRINT : PRINT "VALUE      UNITS"
1630 ND=0
1640 J=7
```

Figure 3.14: Program Listing: Weighted Average (continues)

```
WEIGHTED AVERAGE

ENTER DATA, RETURN WHEN DONE

VALUE        UNITS

? 10         ? 4
? 40         ? 4
? 60         ? 2
?            ?



  WEIGHTED AVERAGE IS :       32



----------------------------------------
WOULD YOU LIKE TO
COMPUTE
AGAIN Y OR N ?
```

Figure 3.13: Screen Display: Weighted Average

```
1650 LOCATE J,1 : PRINT "                        ";
1660 LOCATE J,1    : INPUT D(ND,0)
1670 LOCATE J,12   : INPUT D(ND,1)
1680 IF D(ND,1)=0 THEN 1720
1690 ND=ND+1
1700 J=J+1
1710 IF J=17 THEN 1640 ELSE 1650
1720 REM NOW COMPUTE AND PRINT
1730 AVE=0 : U=0
1740 FOR I = 0 TO ND-1
1750   AVE= AVE+D(I,0)*D(I,1)
1760   U=U+D(I,1)
1770 NEXT I
1780 AVE=AVE/U
1790 LOCATE 16,3
1800 PRINT "WEIGHTED AVERAGE IS : ";
1810 PRINT USING "######,"; AVE
1820 Q2$="COMPUTE"  : GOSUB 3400       'ASK FOR ANOTHER
1830 IF YN$="N" THEN END ELSE GOTO 1590
```

Figure 3.14: Program Listing: Weighted Average

SALESPERSON'S COMMISSION

Description

We will now enter a program to calculate the commission due to a salesperson. You specify the salesperson's monthly draw, monthly sales volume, and commission percentage. A negative result indicates that the salesperson has not sold his quota.

Example

Sam Spade receives a monthly draw of $1,200. He earns 6% commission on the sales he makes as a furniture salesman. What commission is he owed in a month during which he sells $25,000 of furniture? Figures 3.15 and 3.16 are the screen display and the program listing for the Salesperson's Commission program.

□□□

```
SALESPERSON'S COMMISSION

   MONTHLY DRAW  ($)         1,200.00
   MONTHLY SALES ($)        25,000.00
   COMMISSION (%)                6.00

COMMISSION EARNED           $1,500.00
DUE (LESS DRAW)               $300.00










----------------------------------------
WOULD YOU LIKE TO
COMPUTE
AGAIN Y OR N ?
```

Figure 3.15: Screen Display: Salesperson's Commission

```
1840 REM ----------------------------------
1850 N$=      "SALESPERSON'S COMMISSION"
1860 REM ----------------------------------
1870 GOSUB 6200 : K=1
1880 REM GET INPUT PARAMETERS
1890 Q1$="ENTER DATA" : Q2$=""
1900 Q3$="MONTHLY DRAW  ($)"    : GOSUB 6600
1910 Q3$="MONTHLY SALES ($)"    : GOSUB 6600
1920 Q3$="COMMISSION (%) "      : GOSUB 6600
1930 REM COMPUTE AND PRINT
1940 PRINT
1950 PRINT "COMMISSION EARNED ";TAB(24)
1960 PRINT USING "$$####,.##";PAR(2)*PAR(3)/100
1970 PRINT "DUE (LESS DRAW)    ";TAB(24)
1980 PRINT USING "$$####,.##";PAR(2)*PAR(3)/100-PAR(1)
1990 Q2$="COMPUTE"  : GOSUB 3400       'ASK FOR ANOTHER
2000 IF YN$="N" THEN END ELSE GOTO 1840
```

Figure 3.16: Program Listing: Salesperson's Commission

WAGES WITH OVERTIME

Description

This program makes it easy to calculate the total wages due an employee who earns overtime pay at a premium rate. You enter the employee's base hourly pay, the overtime pay factor, and the number of base and overtime hours that the employee worked.

Example

Toni earns $10.00 an hour as a machine operator. During a very busy week she works her regular 40 hours plus 12 hours at overtime pay. You wish to compute her total wages, with overtime paid at time and one half. Figures 3.17 and 3.18 show the results of the overtime computation and the program listing.

□□□

```
WAGES WITH OVERTIME

  BASE RATE  ($/HR)           10.00
  OT PAY FACTOR                1.50
  BASE HOURS WORKED           40.00
  OT HOURS WORKED             12.00

   BASE PAY                 $400.00
   OT PAY                   $180.00
   TOTAL PAY                $580.00




----------------------------------------
WOULD YOU LIKE TO
COMPUTE
AGAIN Y OR N ?
```

Figure 3.17: Screen Display: Wages with Overtime

```
2010 REM ------------------------------
2020 N$=     "WAGES WITH OVERTIME"
2030 REM ------------------------------
2040 GOSUB 6200 : K=1
2050 REM GET INPUT PARAMETERS
2060 Q1$="ENTER DATA" : Q2$=""
2070 Q3$="BASE RATE  ($/HR)"       : GOSUB 6600
2080 Q3$="OT PAY FACTOR"           : GOSUB 6600
2090 Q3$="BASE HOURS WORKED"       : GOSUB 6600
2100 Q3$="OT HOURS WORKED"         : GOSUB 6600
2110 REM COMPUTE AND PRINT
2120 PRINT
2130 PRINT "   BASE PAY ";TAB(24)
2140 PRINT USING "$$####,.##";PAR(1)*PAR(3)
2150 PRINT "   OT PAY   ";TAB(24)
2160 PRINT USING "$$####,.##";PAR(1)*PAR(2)*PAR(4)
2170 PRINT "   TOTAL PAY";TAB(24)
2180 PRINT USING "$$####,.##";PAR(1)*PAR(3)+PAR(1)*PAR(2)*PAR(4)
2190 Q2$="COMPUTE"  : GOSUB 3400      'ASK FOR ANOTHER
2200 IF YN$="N" THEN END ELSE GOTO 2010
```

Figure 3.18: Program Listing: Wages with Overtime

EXECUTIVE DECISION MAKER

Description

When all else fails, you can use this program to assist you in making key business decisions. Simply type your question into the computer. The program uses advanced decision theory to answer your question. (This program is fun to run at a cocktail party or other social gatherings.)

Example

Ed needs to know whether a high-risk project will succeed. Because his staff members cannot provide him with a definite recommendation, he asks his computer, as shown in Figure 3.19. The listing for this program is in Figure 3.20.

□□□

```
EXECUTIVE DECISION MAKER

PLEASE TYPE YOUR QUESTION
=>? WILL THIS PROJECT SUCCEED?
YOU'D BETTER BELIEVE IT









---------------------------------------
WOULD YOU LIKE TO
ASK A QUESTION
AGAIN Y OR N ?
```

Figure 3.19: Screen Display: Executive Decision Maker

```
2210 REM ---------------------------------
2220 N$=     "EXECUTIVE DECISION MAKER"
2230 REM ---------------------------------
2240 GOSUB 6200 : K=1
2250 PRINT "PLEASE TYPE YOUR QUESTION"
2260 PRINT "=>";
2270 INPUT Q$ : Y=LEN(Q$)
2280 IF Y < 6 THEN 2300
2290 Y=INT(Y/2) : GOTO 2280
2300 ON Y GOTO 2310,2320,2330,2340,2350
2310 PRINT "NOT ON YOUR LIFE" : GOTO 2360
2320 PRINT "GO FOR IT !! "    : GOTO 2360
2330 PRINT "YOU'D BETTER BELIEVE IT" : GOTO 2360
2340 PRINT "FLIP A COIN !"    : GOTO 2360
2350 PRINT "MAKE YOUR BREAK- QUICKLY"
2360 Q2$="ASK A QUESTION"  : GOSUB 3400 'ASK FOR ANOTH
2370 IF YN$="N" THEN END ELSE GOTO 2210
```

Figure 3.20: Program Listing: Executive Decision Maker

BUSINESS PROGRAMS MENU

If you save all the programs in this chapter in one tape or diskette file, you can add the menu program shown here to run the other programs. You select the programs by using the number keys of your computer. Remember to replace the END instruction in each program with a RETURN. Review the menu entry instructions in Chapter 2 prior to creating your menu. Figures 3.21 and 3.22 display an image of the menu and the menu selection program.

□□□

```
1 = STRAIGHT-LINE DEPRECIATION
2 = DECLINING-BALANCE DEPRECIATION
3 = SUM-OF-YEARS'-DIGITS DEPRECIATION
4 = BREAK-EVEN POINT
5 = ECONOMIC ORDERING QUANTITIY
6 = SALES PRICE WITH DISCOUNT
7 = WEIGHTED AVERAGE
8 = SALESPERSON'S COMMISSION
9 = WAGES WITH OVERTIME
0 = EXECUTIVE DECISION MAKER




-----------------------------------------

CHOOSE PROGRAM :
```

Figure 3.21: Screen Display: Business Programs Menu

```
100 REM ------------------------------
110 N$=       "BUSINESS PROGRAMS"
120 REM ------------------------------
130 GOSUB 6200                          'INITIALIZE
140 REM SET UP MENU ARRAY
150 X$(1)="STRAIGHT-LINE DEPRECIATION"
160 X$(2)="DECLINING-BALANCE DEPRECIATION"
170 X$(3)="SUM-OF-YEARS'-DIGITS DEPRECIATION"
180 X$(4)="BREAK-EVEN POINT"
190 X$(5)="ECONOMIC ORDERING QUANTITIY"
200 X$(6)="SALES PRICE WITH DISCOUNT"
210 X$(7)="WEIGHTED AVERAGE"
220 X$(8)="SALESPERSON'S COMMISSION"
230 X$(9)="WAGES WITH OVERTIME"
240 X$(10)="EXECUTIVE DECISION MAKER"
250 N=10 : GOSUB 7000                   'DISPLAY MENU
260 ON X GOSUB 280,500,740,990,1140,1310,1550,1840,2010,2210
270 GOTO 100
```

Figure 3.22: Program Listing: Business Programs Menu

□□□□4

REAL ESTATE PROGRAMS

In this chapter we present eight useful real estate programs. These programs allow you to set up mortgage payment schedules and perform many other practical computations.

Two programs in this chapter are especially interesting. You can use the Affordable House Price program to find the sales price of a home that a bank will finance. This program is helpful both in finding a price range you can afford and in negotiating a price should you decide to purchase. Another program you will find particularly enlightening is the Accelerated Payments program. A small increase in your monthly payment can drastically reduce the total interest you pay on a home. Take a look at Figure 4.8, and you'll see what we mean!

As in the other chapters, we provide a menu selection program that you can use to create a set of real estate programs.

REAL ESTATE SUBROUTINES

The programs in this chapter make use of three common subroutines. You should first enter these subroutines and save them on tape or disk. When you are ready to enter a program, load the common subroutines. Then type in the program and save the subroutines and program together as a new tape or disk file. (Merge SUBLIB with this file prior to running your program.) You should enter all the programs in the chapter on the same tape or disk file with these subroutines if you wish to use the menu selection program. The common subroutines are shown in Figure 4.1. These routines are used to get input for a payment calculation, calculate a payment, and compute the remaining balance of a loan.

□□□

```
250 REM ------------------------------
260 REM ROUTINE TO CALCULATE PAYMENT
270 REM ------------------------------
280 REM          CALLING PARAMETERS
290 REM          IN=ANNUAL INTEREST RATE
300 REM          YR=NO OF YEARS
310 REM          AM=AMOUNT OF LOAN
320 REM
330 N1=12*YR :I1=IN/100/12 : V=1/(1+I1) :
340 P=AM*I1/(1-V^N1)
350 RETURN
360 REM ------------------------------
370 REM GET INPUT FOR PAYMENT CALC
380 REM ------------------------------
390 Q1$="SPECIFY PARAMETERS" : Q2$=""
400 Q3$="AMOUNT BORROWED ($)"  :GOSUB 6600
410 Q3$="ANNUAL INT RATE (%) " :GOSUB 6600
420 Q3$="TERM OF LOAN (YRS)"   :GOSUB 6600
430 AM=PAR(1)
440 IN=PAR(2)
450 YR=PAR(3)
460 RETURN
470 REM ------------------------------
480 REM CALCULATE REMAINING BALANCE
490 REM ------------------------------
500 REM      CALLING PARAMETERS
510 REM      P=PAYMENT
520 REM      IN=ANNUAL INTEREST RATE
530 REM      N=PAYMENT NUMBER
540 REM      AM = AMOUNT OF LOAN
550 FOR I= 1 TO N
560     AM= AM-P+IN/12/100*AM
570 NEXT I
580 RETURN
```

Figure 4.1: Program Listing: Real Estate Subroutines

MONTHLY PAYMENT

Description

The monthly payment program finds the monthly payment necessary to fully amortize a loan. You must provide the amount of the loan, the annual interest rate, and the term of the loan in years.

Example

Don and Donna can purchase a house for $100,000. They plan to make a $25,000 down payment and finance the balance at 12% for 30 years. Find their monthly payment. Figures 4.2 and 4.3 show the screen display and the program listing for the monthly payment program.

□□□

```
MONTHLY PAYMENT CALCULATION

  AMOUNT BORROWED ($)   75,000.00
  ANNUAL INT RATE (%)       12.00
  TERM OF LOAN (YRS)        30.00

MONTHLY PAYMENT IS        $771.46




----------------------------------------
WOULD YOU LIKE TO
COMPUTE
AGAIN Y OR N ?
```

Figure 4.2: Screen Display: Monthly Payment

```
590 REM -----------------------------------
600 N$=    "MONTHLY PAYMENT CALCULATION"
610 REM -----------------------------------
620 GOSUB 6200  : K=1                  'INITIALIZE
630 GOSUB 360                          'GET PARAMETERS
640 GOSUB 250                          'CALCULATE PYMT
650 PRINT
660 PRINT "MONTHLY PAYMENT IS";TAB(22)
670 PRINT USING "$$######,.##"; P
680 Q2$="COMPUTE" : GOSUB 3400         'ASK FOR ANOTHER
690 IF YN$="N" THEN END ELSE 620
```

Figure 4.3: Program Listing: Monthly Payment

MORTGAGE SCHEDULE

Description

This program displays a mortgage schedule on the screen for any year you choose. You enter the amount of the loan, the annual interest rate, the term of the loan, and the year for which you wish the mortgage schedule to be displayed. Thus, you can rapidly review the principal and interest you pay in any year. The interest you pay is deductible from your income tax.

Example

The mortgage on Sam and Samantha's home is $60,000. The annual interest rate is 11.5%, and the term of the loan is 25 years. Sam and Samantha would like to review the principal and interest they will be paying during the sixth year of the loan. Figure 4.4 shows the screen display for this example. The program listing is displayed in Figure 4.5.

□□□

```
MORTGAGE SCHEDULE

   AMOUNT BORROWED ($)    60,000.00
   ANNUAL INT RATE (%)        11.50
   TERM OF LOAN (YRS)         25.00
   YEAR                        6.00
        MONTH    PRINCIPAL     INTEREST       BALANCE
        61.00        61.82       548.06     57,127.15
        62.00        62.41       547.47     57,064.73
        63.00        63.01       546.87     57,001.72
        64.00        63.61       546.27     56,938.10
        65.00        64.22       545.66     56,873.88
        66.00        64.84       545.04     56,809.04
        67.00        65.46       544.42     56,743.58
        68.00        66.09       543.79     56,677.49
        69.00        66.72       543.16     56,610.76
        70.00        67.36       542.52     56,543.40
        71.00        68.01       541.87     56,475.39
        72.00        68.66       541.22     56,406.73
----------------------------------------
WOULD YOU LIKE TO
COMPUTE
AGAIN Y OR N ?
```

Figure 4.4: Screen Display: Mortgage Schedule

```
700 REM ------------------------------
710 N$=      "MORTGAGE SCHEDULE"
720 REM ------------------------------
730 GOSUB 6200   : K=1                  'INITIALIZE
740 GOSUB 360                           'GET LOAN PARAMETERS
750 Q3$="YEAR"
760 GOSUB 6600   :N=PAR(4)              'GET YEAR
770 GOSUB 250                           'CALCULATE PAYMENT
780 N=12*N-12                           'COMPUTE FIRST MONTH
790 GOSUB 470                           'GET BEGINNING BALANCE
800 PRINT "        MONTH    PRINCIPAL     INTEREST      BALANCE"
810 FOR J=1 TO 12
820   I1=IN/12/100*AM  :  P1=P-I1  :AM=AM-P1 'COMPUTE P & I
830   PRINT USING "########,.##";N+1,P1,I1,AM
840   N=N+1
850 NEXT J
860 Q2$="COMPUTE"  :  GOSUB 3400
870 IF YN$="N" THEN END ELSE 700
```

Figure 4.5: Program Listing: Mortgage Schedule

REMAINING BALANCE OF A LOAN

Description

This program finds the remaining balance on a loan. You can run this program to calculate the amount due should you choose to pay off the loan. The program assumes that all prior payments have been the exact monthly payment. To use the program you specify the amount of the mortgage, the interest rate and length of the loan, and the payment number for which you want to determine the remaining balance. Don't be concerned if this program takes a while to display its answer.

Example

John's mortgage is $90,000. His loan is for 30 years at an annual interest rate of 9%. He would like to compute the loan balance at the end of five years (the sixtieth payment). Figures 4.6 and 4.7 show the screen display and the program listing for the Remaining Balance program.

□□□

```
REMAINING BALANCE

  AMOUNT BORROWED ($)   90,000.00
  ANNUAL INT RATE (%)        9.00
  TERM OF LOAN (YRS)        30.00
  PAYMENT NUMBER            60.00

MONTHLY PAYMENT           $724.16
BAL AFTER  60  PMTS    $86,292.20





---------------------------------------
WOULD YOU LIKE TO
COMPUTE
AGAIN Y OR N ?
```

Figure 4.6: Screen Display: Remaining Balance of a Loan

```
880 REM ------------------------------
890 N$=       "REMAINING BALANCE"
900 REM ------------------------------
910 GOSUB 6200   : K=1             'INITIALIZE
920 GOSUB 360                      'GET LOAN PARAMETERS
930 Q3$="PAYMENT NUMBER"
940 GOSUB 6600   :N=PAR(4)         'GET PAYMENT NO.
950 GOSUB 250                      'CALCULATE PAYMENT
960 GOSUB 470                      'COMPUTE BALANCE
970 PRINT
980 PRINT "MONTHLY PAYMENT";TAB(22);
990 PRINT USING "$$######,.##";P
1000 PRINT "BAL AFTER ";N; " PMTS"; TAB(22);
1010 PRINT USING "$$######,.##";AM
1020 Q2$="COMPUTE" : GOSUB 3400   'ASK FOR ANOTHER
1030 IF YN$="N" THEN END ELSE 880
```

Figure 4.7: Program Listing: Remaining Balance of a Loan

EFFECT OF ACCELERATED PAYMENTS

Description

You will find this program extremely useful—it allows you to find the effect of increasing the monthly payments on your mortgage. An increase in the monthly payments will reduce both the number of years of payments and the total interest you pay. To use this program, enter the amount of the loan, the annual interest rate, the length of the loan, the year in which you increase the payments, and the extra amount you will pay each month. This program computes as many times as is necessary to reduce the loan balance to zero, so you may find that it takes a while for the answer to appear.

Example

Cindy has decided to increase the monthly payments on her home loan by $100 each month. She begins the increased payments in the seventh year of the loan and would like to know how much she will save on the interest. Her loan is for $60,000 at 9.75%; the term of her loan is 30 years. You can see in Figure 4.8 that Cindy will save $41,000 with this increase in her monthly payment. Figure 4.9 shows the program listing for the Accelerated Payments program.

```
1040 REM ------------------------------
1050 N$=     "ACCELERATED PAYMENTS"
1060 REM ------------------------------
1070 GOSUB 6200 : K=1                    'INITIALIZE
1080 GOSUB 360                           'GET LOAN PARAMETERS
1090 Q3$="YEAR OF INCREASE "
1100 GOSUB 6600   :N=PAR(4)              'GET YEAR
1110 GOSUB 250                           'CALCULATE PAYMENT
1120 N=12*N-12                           'COMPUTE FIRST MONTH
1130 Q3$="EXTRA AMOUNT PAID ($)"
1140 GOSUB 6600 : EX=PAR(5)              'GET EXTRA
1150 REM COMPUTE PRIN INT AND BAL TO DATE
1160 TI=0 : BAL=0 : TP=0
1170 FOR J=1 TO N
1180      I1=IN/12/100*AM : P1=P-I1 : AM=AM-P1
1190      TI= TI+I1 : TP=TP+P1
1200 NEXT J
```

Figure 4.9: Program Listing: Effect of Accelerated Payments (continues)

```
ACCELERATED PAYMENTS

  AMOUNT BORROWED ($)     60,000.00
  ANNUAL INT RATE (%)          9.75
  TERM OF LOAN (YRS)          30.00
  YEAR OF INCREASE             7.00
  EXTRA AMOUNT PAID ($)      100.00

YEARS TO PAY OFF              20.58
TOTAL INTEREST PAID      $84,431.84
INTEREST SAVED           $41,144.44

----------------------------------------
WOULD YOU LIKE TO
COMPUTE
AGAIN Y OR N ?
```

Figure 4.8: Screen Display: Effect of Accelerated Payments

```
1210 REM COMPUTE INTEREST WITH NO INCREASE
1220 TI2=0 : AM2=PAR(1)
1230 FOR J=1 TO 12*YR
1240   I2=IN/12/100*AM2 : P2=P-I2 : AM2=AM2-P2
1250   TI2=TI2+I2
1260 NEXT J
1270 REM COMPUTE WITH XTRA PAYMENT
1280 J=0
1290 I1=IN/12/100*AM: TI=TI+I1
1300 P1=P+EX-I1 : TP=TP+P1
1310 AM=AM-P1
1320 J=J+1
1330 IF AM >0 THEN 1290
1340 PRINT
1350 PRINT "YEARS TO PAY OFF";TAB(25);
1360 PRINT USING "######.##";PAR(4)+J/12-1
1370 PRINT "TOTAL INTEREST PAID";TAB(22);
1380 PRINT USING "$$######,.##";TI
1390 PRINT "INTEREST SAVED";TAB(22);
1400 PRINT USING "$$######,.##";TI2-TI
1410 Q2$="COMPUTE" : GOSUB 3400
1420 IF YN$="N" THEN END ELSE 1040
```

Figure 4.9: Program Listing: Effect of Accelerated Payments

BALLOON PAYMENT CALCULATION

Description

Many recent mortgages have been set up with a balloon payment due at the end of a specified period. This program allows you to calculate the required balloon payment. You must enter the amount of the loan, the annual interest rate, the term of the loan, and the year in which the balloon payment is due.

Example

Max has a mortgage for $125,000. The annual interest rate is 11%. The payments are amortized over 30 years; Max must pay off the entire loan at the end of 10 years. What will be the amount of Max's balloon payment? Figures 4.10 and 4.11 show the screen display and the program listing for the Balloon Payment program.

□□□

```
BALLOON PAYMENT

  AMOUNT BORROWED ($)  125,000.00
  ANNUAL INT RATE (%)       11.00
  TERM OF LOAN (YRS)        30.00
  YEAR LOAN DUE             10.00

MONTHLY PAYMENT         $1,190.40

BALLOON PAYMENT
AFTER  10  YEARS      $115,327.70





----------------------------------------
WOULD YOU LIKE TO
COMPUTE
AGAIN Y OR N ?
```

Figure 4.10: Screen Display: Balloon Payment Calculation

```
1430 REM ------------------------------
1440 N$=       "BALLOON PAYMENT"
1450 REM ------------------------------
1460 GOSUB 6200  : K=1          'INITIALIZE
1470 GOSUB 360                  'GET LOAN PARAMETERS
1480 Q3$="YEAR LOAN DUE"
1490 GOSUB 6600  :N=12*PAR(4)   'GET YEAR DUE
1500 GOSUB 250                  'CALCULATE PAYMENT
1510 GOSUB 470                  'COMPUTE BALANCE
1520 PRINT
1530 PRINT "MONTHLY PAYMENT";TAB(22);
1540 PRINT USING "$$######,.##";P
1550 PRINT : PRINT "BALLOON PAYMENT"
1560 PRINT "AFTER ";N/12; " YEARS"; TAB(22);
1570 PRINT USING "$$######,.##";AM
1580 Q2$="COMPUTE" : GOSUB 3400       'ASK FOR ANOTHER
1590 IF YN$="N" THEN END ELSE 1430
```

Figure 4.11: Program Listing: Balloon Payment Calculation

AFFORDABLE HOUSE PRICE

Description

You can use this program to find the price of a home for which a bank will give you a loan. This program can be invaluable when you are negotiating to buy a new home. To use the program, enter the annual interest rate and term of available loans, your annual income, the estimated annual taxes and insurance, the percent of your gross income that the bank will allow for your total monthly payments, and the percent down payment you will make.

Example

Bill and Betty would like to purchase a new home. The available interest rate for home loans is 13.5% for 30-year loans. The couple's annual income is $50,000 per year, and they plan to put 20% down on their new house. Bill and Betty estimate that their yearly taxes and insurance will be $2,400. Their banker has told them that the monthly payment on their house must not exceed 35% of their monthly income. Figures 4.12 and 4.13 are the screen display and the program listing for the Affordable House Price program.

□□□

```
AFFORDABLE HOUSE PRICE

  ANNUAL INT RATE (%)          13.50
  TERM OF LOAN (YRS)           30.00
  BUYERS ANNUAL INC        50,000.00
  EST ANNUAL TAX & INS      2,400.00
  % OF INC FOR PAYMENTS        35.00
  % DOWN PAYMENT               20.00

AMOUNT FINANCED          $109,858.60
AFFORDABLE HOUSE         $137,323.20




----------------------------------------
WOULD YOU LIKE TO
COMPUTE
AGAIN Y OR N ?
```

Figure 4.12: Screen Display: Affordable House Price

```
1600 REM -----------------------------
1610 N$=   "AFFORDABLE HOUSE PRICE"
1620 REM -----------------------------
1630 GOSUB 6200 : K=1                      'INITIALIZE
1640 Q1$="SPECIFY PARAMETERS" : Q2$=""
1650 Q3$="ANNUAL INT RATE (%) "   : GOSUB 6600
1660 Q3$="TERM OF LOAN (YRS)"     : GOSUB 6600
1670 Q3$="BUYERS ANNUAL INC"      : GOSUB 6600
1680 Q3$="EST ANNUAL TAX & INS"   : GOSUB 6600
1690 Q3$="% OF INC FOR PAYMENTS"  : GOSUB 6600
1700 Q3$="% DOWN PAYMENT"         : GOSUB 6600
1710 PRINT
1720 REM COMPUTE ALLOWABLE PAYMENT
1730 P=PAR(5)/100*PAR(3)/12 - PAR(4)/12
1740 REM COMPUTE AMOUNT FINANCED
1750 IN=PAR(1)/100/12 :N1=12*PAR(2) : V=1/(1+IN)
1760 AM=P*(1-V^N1)/IN
1770 PRINT "AMOUNT FINANCED";TAB(22);
1780 PRINT USING "$$######,.##";AM
1790 PRINT "AFFORDABLE HOUSE"; TAB(22);
1800 PRINT USING "$$######,.##";AM/(1-PAR(6)/100)
1810 Q2$="COMPUTE" : GOSUB 3400
1820 IF YN$="N" THEN END ELSE 1600
```

Figure 4.13: Program Listing: Affordable House Price

MORTGAGE WITH SECOND MORTGAGE

Description

We shall now examine a program you can use to find the total payments on a house that will have both a first and second mortgage. To use this program you enter the purchase price of the home, the cash available for a down payment, and the amount of the first mortgage you will obtain. You also specify the interest rate of the first and second mortgages and the length of the first. We assume that the second mortgage is paid monthly on an interest-only basis.

Example

Joanne has saved $20,000 for a down payment on a new house. The house will cost $140,000 and she plans to take out a first mortgage for $90,000. The first mortgage will be for 30 years at 12% annual interest. She will also have a 16% interest-only second mortgage. What will be her total payments? The resulting screen display for this example is shown in Figure 4.14; the program listing appears in Figure 4.15.

```
1830 REM ----------------------------
1840 N$=    "MORTGAGE WITH SECOND"
1850 REM ----------------------------
1860 GOSUB 6200 : K=1
1870 Q1$="SPECIFY PARAMETERS" : Q2$=""
1880 Q3$="PURCHASE PRICE ($)"   : GOSUB 6600
1890 Q3$="CASH AVAILABLE ($)"   : GOSUB 6600
1900 Q3$="FIRST MORT ($)"       : GOSUB 6600
1910 Q3$="FIRST RATE (%)"       : GOSUB 6600
1920 Q3$="FIRST TERM (YRS)"     : GOSUB 6600
1930 Q3$="SECOND RATE (%)"      : GOSUB 6600
```

Figure 4.15: Program Listing: Mortgage with Second Mortgage (continues)

```
MORTGAGE WITH SECOND

  PURCHASE PRICE ($)   140,000.00
  CASH AVAILABLE ($)    20,000.00
  FIRST MORT ($)        90,000.00
  FIRST RATE (%)            12.00
  FIRST TERM (YRS)          30.00
  SECOND RATE (%)           16.00

PAYMENT (FIRST)           $925.75
PAYMENT (SECOND)          $400.00
TOTAL PAYMENTS          $1,325.75




----------------------------------------
WOULD YOU LIKE TO
COMPUTE
AGAIN Y OR N ?
```

Figure 4.14: Screen Display: Mortgage with Second Mortgage

```
1940 PRINT
1950 AM=PAR(3) : IN=PAR(4) : YR=PAR(5)
1960 REM COMPUTE FIRST PAYMENT
1970 GOSUB 250
1980 PRINT "PAYMENT (FIRST)";TAB(22);
1990 PRINT USING "$$######,.##";P
2000 REM COMPUTE 2ND PAYMENT
2010 IF PAR(2) < PAR(1)-PAR(3) THEN GOTO 2040
2020    PRINT "SECOND MORTGAGE NOT REQUIRED"
2030    GOTO 2090
2040 PRINT "PAYMENT (SECOND)";TAB(22)
2050 P2=(PAR(1)-PAR(2)-PAR(3))*PAR(6)/100/12
2060 PRINT USING "$$######,.##";P2
2070 PRINT "TOTAL PAYMENTS";TAB(22);
2080 PRINT USING "$$######,.##";P+P2
2090 Q2$="COMPUTE" : GOSUB 3400
2100 IF YN$="N" THEN END ELSE 1830
```

Figure 4.15: Program Listing: Mortgage with Second Mortgage

RENTAL PROPERTY ANALYSIS

Description

Let's now consider a program that is very useful for analyzing real estate investments. You can use the Rental Property Analysis program to find the monthly payment and cash flow on a rental property. (We don't consider the after-tax effects of depreciation.) You must enter the amount of the loan on your rental property, the annual interest rate and length of the loan, and the annual insurance, taxes, and maintenance. You must also enter the monthly rental income.

Example

Herb is planning to purchase a house, which he will rent for $475 per month. The first mortgage will be $80,000, amortized over 30 years at 12% interest. Herb estimates that the annual insurance will be $500, the property taxes $1,600, and the maintenance $400. What will be his monthly payment and cash flow? Figures 4.16 and 4.17 are the screen display and program listing for this example.

□□□

```
RENTAL PROPERTY ANALYSIS

  AMOUNT BORROWED ($)      80,000.00
  ANNUAL INT RATE (%)          12.00
  TERM OF LOAN (YRS)           30.00
  ANNUAL INSURANCE ($)        500.00
  ANNUAL TAXES ($)          1,600.00
  ANNUAL MAINT ($)            400.00
  MONTHLY INCOME ($)          475.00

MONTHLY PAYMENT IS           $822.89
MONTHLY CASH FLOW           -$556.22




----------------------------------------
WOULD YOU LIKE TO
COMPUTE
AGAIN Y OR N ?
```

Figure 4.16: Screen Display: Rental Property Analysis

```
2110 REM ------------------------------
2120 N$=  "RENTAL PROPERTY ANALYSIS"
2130 REM ------------------------------
2140 GOSUB 6200 : K=1
2150 REM GET PARAMETERS
2160 GOSUB 360
2170 Q3$="ANNUAL INSURANCE ($)" : GOSUB 6600
2180 Q3$="ANNUAL TAXES ($)"     : GOSUB 6600
2190 Q3$="ANNUAL MAINT ($)"     : GOSUB 6600
2200 Q3$="MONTHLY INCOME ($)"   : GOSUB 6600
2210 GOSUB 250                          'CALCULATE PYMT
2220 PRINT
2230 PRINT "MONTHLY PAYMENT IS";TAB(22);
2240 PRINT USING "$$######,.##";P
2250 PRINT "MONTHLY CASH FLOW";TAB(22);
2260 CF=PAR(7)-P-(PAR(4)+PAR(5)+PAR(6))/12
2270 PRINT USING "$$######,.##";CF
2280 Q2$="COMPUTE" : GOSUB 3400
2290 IF YN$="N" THEN END ELSE 2110
```

Figure 4.17: Program Listing: Rental Property Analysis

REAL ESTATE PROGRAMS MENU

We can again combine the programs in this chapter to provide a menu-driven real estate analysis package. The menu display and its program listing are shown in Figures 4.18 and 4.19. Remember to replace the END command in each program with a RETURN command. Instructions for combining and saving the menu program are in Chapter 2.

□□□

```
1 = MONTHLY PAYMENT
2 = MORTGAGE SCHEDULE
3 = REMAINING BALANCE OF LOAN
4 = EFFECT OF ACCELERATED PAYMENTS
5 = BALLOON PAYMENT CALCULATION
6 = AFFORDABLE HOUSE PRICE
7 = MORTGAGE WITH SECOND
8 = RENTAL PROPERTY




----------------------------------------

CHOOSE PROGRAM :
```

Figure 4.18: Screen Display: Real Estate Programs Menu

```
100 REM ------------------------------
110 N$=      "REAL ESTATE PROGRAMS"
120 REM ------------------------------
130 GOSUB 6200                              'INITIALIZE
140 X$(1)="MONTHLY PAYMENT"
150 X$(2)="MORTGAGE SCHEDULE"
160 X$(3)="REMAINING BALANCE OF LOAN"
170 X$(4)="EFFECT OF ACCELERATED PAYMENTS"
180 X$(5)="BALLOON PAYMENT CALCULATION"
190 X$(6)="AFFORDABLE HOUSE PRICE"
200 X$(7)="MORTGAGE WITH SECOND"
210 X$(8)="RENTAL PROPERTY"
220 N=8 : GOSUB 7000                        'DISPLAY MENU
230 ON X GOSUB 590,700,880,1040,1430,1600,1830,2110
240 GOTO 100
```

Figure 4.19: Program Listing: Real Estate Programs Menu

□□□□□5

DATA ANALYSIS PROGRAMS

This chapter describes a set of data analysis programs that you can use to reduce and plot various kinds of data. We present programs that input data, plot it on the screen, compute moving averages, and perform linear regression analyses. The Plot Data program will also plot data that are reduced by the programs in this chapter.

Investors, among others, will find the data analysis programs very useful. You can input daily stock prices and then try the various smoothing programs. These programs smooth out daily price variations and give an indication of longer term trends. The data analysis programs can also be used in many other situations, including analyzing scientific data, plotting and smoothing weight variations, and tracking weather data.

The programs in this and the following two chapters require that you first enter the menu program and additional common subroutines. You should save these programs in one file after they are entered; you then add the other programs as described in Chapter 1. Because the programs in these chapters *begin* with the menu program, you don't have to change any lines within the programs to activate the menu.

DATA ANALYSIS PROGRAMS MENU

The data analysis programs all work together through common arrays and a common menu program. Notice that the menu lists an input program, a plot program, and several analysis programs. You use the programs together by first entering data with the input program. You can then plot the data or analyze it. Input data are stored in the array D. Data you reduce with the analysis programs are stored in the array R.

After you run each program you return to the menu. You can then analyze the data again with a different program; you can plot input data, reduced data, or both; or you can enter new data.

Figure 5.1 shows the screen display of the Data Analysis Menu. Figure 5.2 shows the menu program listing.

□□□

```
1 = INPUT DATA
2 = PLOT DATA
3 = MEAN AND STANDARD DEVIATION
4 = 3-POINT MOVING AVERAGE
5 = WEIGHTED MOVING AVERAGE
6 = 4-POINT CENTERED AVERAGE
7 = LINEAR REGRESSION




----------------------------------------

CHOOSE PROGRAM :
```

Figure 5.1: Screen Display: Data Analysis Menu

```
100 REM ------------------------------
110 N$=    "DATA ANALYSIS PROGRAMS"
120 REM ------------------------------
130 OPTION BASE 1            'SET UP ARRAY SUBSCRIPTS
140 DIM P(80),R(80),D(80)
150 GOSUB 4200               'INITIALIZE
160 REM SET UP MENU
170 X$(1)="INPUT DATA"
180 X$(2)="PLOT DATA"
190 X$(3)="MEAN AND STANDARD DEVIATION"
200 X$(4)="3-POINT MOVING AVERAGE"
210 X$(5)="WEIGHTED MOVING AVERAGE"
220 X$(6)="4-POINT CENTERED AVERAGE"
230 X$(7)="LINEAR REGRESSION"
240 N=7 : GOSUB 7000         'DISPLAY MENU
250 ON X GOSUB 690,920,1140,1360,1560,1760,1960
260 GOTO 150
```

Figure 5.2: Program Listing: Data Analysis Menu

DATA ANALYSIS SUBROUTINES

The Plot Data program uses two subroutines to plot data on the screen. One routine draws the axes; the other scales and plots the data. You must enter these programs prior to using the plot program. Figure 5.3 is the program listing for the axis subroutine. The axis program is set up to work with either a 40-column or an 80-column monitor. Don't enter more than 40 points unless you have an 80-column monitor.

Figure 5.4 shows the program listing for the routine that scales and plots the data. This program plots either input data, reduced data, or both input and reduced data, depending on the user-controlled variable CH$.

□□□

```
270 REM ------------------------------
280 REM DRAW AXES
290 REM ------------------------------
300 CLS
310 FOR I=1 TO 21                          'Y AXIS
320   LOCATE I,6 : PRINT " I"
330 NEXT I
340 FOR I=1 TO 16 STEP 5                   'Y AXIS SCALE
350  LOCATE I,6 : PRINT"-"
360  LOCATE I,1
365  PRINT USING "####"; MX-(MX-MN)/4*(I-1)/5
370 NEXT I
380 LOCATE 21,8
390 FOR I= 1 TO 32                         'X AXIS
400   PRINT "-";
410 NEXT I
420 FOR I=8 TO 38 STEP 5                   'X AXIS TICKS
430   LOCATE 21,I : PRINT "I";
440   LOCATE 22,I-1 : PRINT I-7
450 NEXT I
460 RETURN
```

Figure 5.3: Program Listing: Axis Subroutine

```
470 REM ------------------------------
480 REM SCALE DATA AND PLOT IT
490 REM ------------------------------
500 FOR I= 1 TO ND
510   P1=21-INT(20*(D(I)-MN)/(MX-MN))
520   P2=21-INT(20*(R(I)-MN)/(MX-MN))
530 IF CH$ <> "I" THEN 570
540   IF P1 > 21 OR P1 < 1  THEN GOTO 670
550   LOCATE P1,I+8 : PRINT "*"
560   GOTO 650
570 IF CH$ <> "R" THEN 610
580   IF P2 > 21 OR P2 < 1  THEN GOTO 670
590   LOCATE P2,I+8 : PRINT "+"
600   GOTO 650
610 REM MUST BE BOTH PLOTS
620   IF P1 > 21 OR P1 < 1 OR P2 > 21 OR P2 < 1 THEN 670
630   LOCATE P1,I+8 : PRINT "*"
640   LOCATE P2,I+8 : PRINT "+"
650 NEXT I
660 RETURN
670 ERF=1 : RETURN
680 RETURN
```

Figure 5.4: Program Listing: Scale and Plot Subroutine

INPUT DATA

Description

You use this program to enter data that the other programs analyze and plot. You can enter up to 80 data points with the Input Data program. The data are stored in the array D(I). The program prompts you to enter data in the order of their occurrence. You type a D to signify that you are done entering data. The input screen is set up to display the last ten points that you enter, so you can check yourself as you go along. Remember, all data that you smooth and plot must first be entered with the Input Data program.

Example

Mary Ann would like to input the data she obtained in a laboratory experiment. The data are as follows:

Point	1	2	3	4	5	6	7	8	9	10
Data	1	3	5	4	4	5	7	8	9	11
Point	11	12	13	14	15	16	17	18	19	20
Data	12	15	13	14	15	16	15	13	12	12
Point	21	22	23	24	25	26	27	28	29	30
Data	11	10	7	9	8	7	5	5	4	3
Point	31	32								
Data	3	0								

Figure 5.5 shows the screen display; Figure 5.6 contains the program listing for the Input Data program.

□□□

```
INPUT DATA



     VALUE  11        ? 12
     VALUE  12        ? 15
     VALUE  13        ? 13
     VALUE  14        ? 14
     VALUE  15        ? 15
     VALUE  16        ?
     VALUE  7         ? 7
     VALUE  8         ? 8
     VALUE  9         ? 9
     VALUE  10        ? 11



-----------------------------------------
TYPE IN DATA VALUES IN ORDER
TYPE D WHEN DONE
```

Figure 5.5: Screen Display: Input Data

```
690 REM ------------------------------
700 N$=          "INPUT DATA"
710 REM ------------------------------
720 REM THIS PROGRAM ACCEPTS UP TO 80 DATA VALUES
730 GOSUB 6200                       'INITIALIZE
740 Q1$="TYPE IN DATA VALUES IN ORDER"
750 Q2$="TYPE D WHEN DONE"
760 Q3$=""    : GOSUB 5000           'DIALOG
770 ND=0                             'NO. OF DATA POINTS
780 J=6
790 FOR I= 1 TO 80
800   LOCATE J,10
810   PRINT "                 "      'BLANK LINE
820   LOCATE J,5
830   PRINT "VALUE ";I; TAB(20);
840   INPUT D$
850   IF D$="D" OR D$="d" THEN 910
860   ND=ND+1                        'COUNT DATA POINTS
870   D(I)=VAL(D$)                   'STORE DATA
880   J=J+1
890   IF J=16 THEN J=6               'RESET POINTER
900 NEXT I
910 RETURN
```

Figure 5.6: Program Listing: Input Data

PLOT DATA

Description

The Plot Data program plots either input data or reduced data on the screen. (Reduced data result from using the data analysis programs that follow.) Because you do not need a graphics adapter board to run this program, the resulting plots have poor but usable vertical resolution. You must tell the program to plot input data, reduced data (data on which you have run one of the data analysis programs), or both by answering the program prompt with an I, R, or B respectively. The * symbol represents input data, and the + symbol represents reduced data. You must also specify the maximum and minimum Y-axis scale values. If your input data exceed your scale values, you will get the message DATA OUT OF RANGE. You must then respecify the scale values.

Example

Let's now plot the input data from the previous example. In this case we choose a maximum value of 20 and a minimum value of 0. We choose to plot input data (I), because we have not reduced it yet. Figure 5.7 shows the screen display for the data plot. Figure 5.8 displays the Plot Data program listing.

□□□

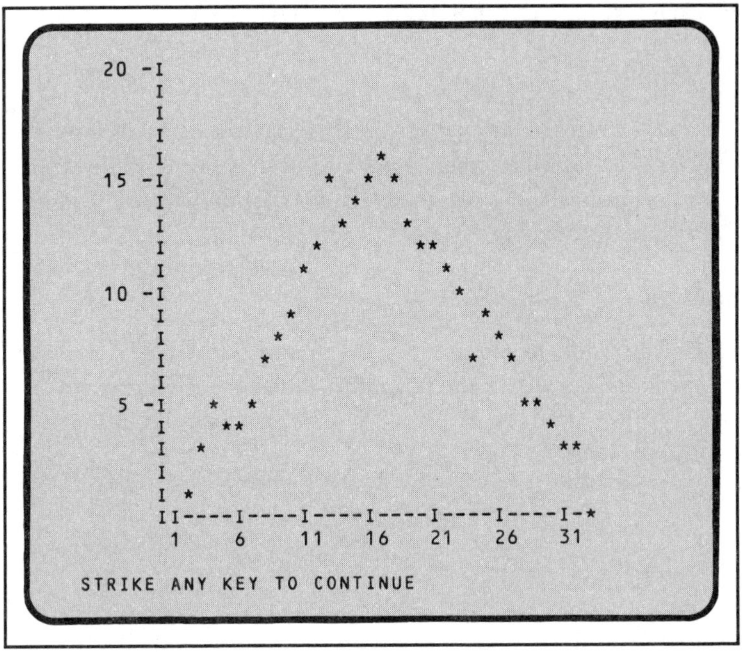

Figure 5.7: Screen Display: Plot Data

```
920 REM ------------------------------
930 N$=       "PLOT DATA ROUTINE"
940 REM ------------------------------
950 Q2$="INPUT OR REDUCED OR BOTH"
955 Q3$="DATA (I OR R OR B)"
960 GOSUB 5000
970 GOSUB 5400                      'GET CHAR
980 IF CH$ ="I" OR CH$ ="R" OR CH$="B" THEN 990 ELSE 970
990 Q1$="" : Q2$=""
1000 Q3$="CHOOSE MAX SCALE : "
1010 GOSUB 5000 : INPUT MX
1020 Q3$="CHOOSE MIN SCALE : "
1030 GOSUB 5000 : INPUT MN
1040 GOSUB 270                      'DRAW AXES
1050 ERF=0
1060 GOSUB 470                      'PLOT DATA
1070 IF ERF <>1 THEN 1110           'OUT OF RANGE ERROR
1080 Q1$="DATA OUT OF RANGE"
1090 Q2$="PLEASE RESPECIFY" :BEEP
1100 GOTO 1000
1110 LOCATE 24,1
1120 PRINT "STRIKE ANY KEY TO CONTINUE";
1130 CH$=INKEY$ :IF CH$="" THEN 1130 ELSE RETURN
```

Figure 5.8: Program Listing: Plot Data

MEAN AND STANDARD DEVIATION

Description

We shall now look at a program that computes the mean and standard deviation for data that have been input with the Input Data program. To use this program you simply select it from the Data Analysis Menu.

Example

Mary Ann would like to compute the mean and standard deviation for the laboratory data she has input. She runs the program and displays the results in Figure 5.9. The program listing for this example appears in Figure 5.10.

□□□

```
MEAN AND STANDARD DEVIATION

MEAN OF INPUT DATA         8.31
STANDARD DEVIATION         4.48











------------------------------------------
STRIKE ANY KEY TO CONTINUE
```

Figure 5.9: Screen Display: Mean and Standard Deviation

```
1140 REM ----------------------------------------
1150 N$=      "MEAN AND STANDARD DEVIATION"
1160 REM ----------------------------------------
1170 GOSUB 6200
1180 REM COMPUTE THE MEAN
1190 ME=0
1200 FOR I = 1 TO ND
1210     ME=ME+D(I)
1220 NEXT I
1230 ME=ME/ND
1240 REM COMPUTE STANDARD DEVIATION
1250 SD=0
1260 FOR I=1 TO ND
1270     SD=SD+(D(I)-ME)^2
1280 NEXT I
1290 SD=(SD/ND)^.5
1300 PRINT "MEAN OF INPUT DATA";TAB(20);
1310 PRINT USING "######,.##"; ME
1320 PRINT "STANDARD DEVIATION";TAB(20);
1330 PRINT USING "######,.##";SD
1340 GOSUB 7400
1350 RETURN
```

Figure 5.10: Program Listing: Mean and Standard Deviation

THREE-POINT MOVING AVERAGE

Description

We shall now present three data smoothing programs. The first program computes a three-point moving average on data you store in the Input Data array. The smoothed data are stored in the array R(I). You can display the smoothed data in either numeric or graph form. The three-point moving average takes the average value of the three prior data points and uses the average as the smoothed result. After the program smooths the data it will ask

```
DO YOU WANT TO PRINT THE DATA
```

If you answer with a Y, the program displays the data in numeric form. When you return to the main menu, you can graph the smoothed data wih the Plot Data program. If you answer with an N, the program returns immediately to the main menu, so that you can run the Plot Data program.

Example

Mary Ann would like to try various smoothing techniques on her laboratory data. She first runs the Three-Point Moving Average program and graphs the results together with the input data. You can see the smoothed data in Figure 5.11; wherever the input data and smoothed data are the same, only the smoothed data are shown. The program listing is shown in Figure 5.12.

□□□

```
20 -I
    I
    I
    I
    I                *
15 -I            *  * ++
    I              *++  +
    I             *+   * +
    I           * +     **+
    I          *          *++
10 -I            +         *
    I         * +            +
    I        * +              +++
    I       *               *  *
    I         +                  +
 5 -I   *  * +                  **+
    I    *+++                     **+
    I  * +                         **+
    I
    I *
    II+++-I----I----I----I----I----I-*
     1    6    11   16   21   26   31

STRIKE ANY KEY TO CONTINUE
```

Figure 5.11: Screen Display: Three-Point Moving Average

```
1360 REM ------------------------------
1370 N$=    "3-POINT MOVING AVERAGE"
1380 REM ------------------------------
1390 GOSUB 6200                            'INITIALIZE
1400 REM SET UP THE RESULT IN R(I)
1410 R(1)=0 : R(2)=0 : R(3)=0
1420 FOR I = 4 TO ND
1430   R(I)=(D(I-3)+D(I-2)+D(I-1))/3
1440 NEXT I
1450 Q1$="DO YOU WANT TO PRINT THE"
1460 Q2$="DATA  (Y OR N)"
1470 Q3$="" : GOSUB 5000
1480 GOSUB 7800                            'ASK YES OR NO
1490 IF YN$="N" THEN RETURN
1500 CLS
1510 FOR I = 4 TO ND
1520   PRINT R(I),
1530 NEXT I
1540 GOSUB 7400                            'WAIT FOR KEY
1550 RETURN
```

Figure 5.12: Program Listing: Three-Point Moving Average

WEIGHTED MOVING AVERAGE

Description

A second smoothing technique is the three-point weighted average. We smooth the data by weighting the most recent point by three, the second most recent point by two, and the third most recent point by one. Thus, the most recent point is given the highest weight. You use this program by calling it from the menu; the resulting data are stored in the array R(I). Again, the data can be displayed numerically or graphed by the Plot Data program. Note that only one set of reduced data can be stored at a time.

Example

Let's use the weighted average program with Mary Ann's laboratory data. In Figure 5.13 we plot both the input data and the reduced data resulting from the Weighted Moving Average program. The program listing is given in Figure 5.14.

□□□

```
20 -I
    I
    I
    I
    I                *
15 -I            *  * ++
    I              * +  +
    I             +++  *
    I           *       *++
    I          * +        *+
10 -I                      *+
    I         * +            *
    I        * +             +++
    I       * +             *  *+
    I                            +
 5 -I   *  * +                  **+
    I    *+++                     *+
    I  * +                         *++
    I
    I *
    II+++-I----I----I----I----I----I-*
     1    6    11   16   21   26   31

STRIKE ANY KEY TO CONTINUE
```

Figure 5.13: Screen Display: Weighted Moving Average

```
1560 REM ---------------------------------
1570 N$=  "3-PT. WEIGHTED MOVING AVERAGE"
1580 REM ---------------------------------
1590 GOSUB 6200                          'INITIALIZE
1600 REM SET UP THE RESULT IN R(I)
1610 R(1)=0 : R(2)=0 : R(3)=0
1620 FOR I = 4 TO ND
1630   R(I)=(D(I-3)+2*D(I-2)+3*D(I-1))/6
1640 NEXT I
1650 Q1$="DO YOU WANT TO PRINT THE"
1660 Q2$="DATA  (Y OR N)"
1670 Q3$="" : GOSUB 5000
1680 GOSUB 7800                          'ASK YES OR NO
1690 IF YN$="N" THEN RETURN
1700 CLS
1710 FOR I = 4 TO ND
1720   PRINT R(I),
1730 NEXT I
1740 GOSUB 7400                          'WAIT FOR KEY
1750 RETURN
```

Figure 5.14: Program Listing: Weighted Moving Average

FOUR-POINT CENTERED AVERAGE

Description

We now review a final smoothing technique, the four-point centered average. This technique weights the first and fifth most recent points by a factor of one and the second, third, and fourth most recent points by a factor of two. You use this program by selecting it from the menu. You can list the smoothed data or plot it with the Plot Data program.

Example

Let's apply the centered-average technique to Mary Ann's laboratory data. Figure 5.15 shows the smoothed data along with the input data. Figure 5.16 shows the program listing.

□□□

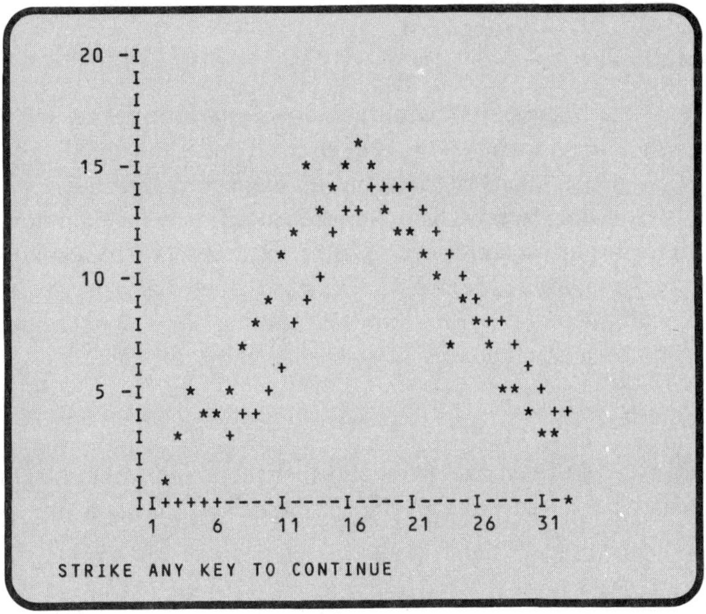

Figure 5.15: Screen Display: Four-Point Centered Average

```
1760 REM ------------------------------
1770 N$=   "4-PT. CENTERED  AVERAGE"
1780 REM ------------------------------
1790 GOSUB 6200                              'INITIALIZE
1800 REM SET UP THE RESULT IN R(I)
1810 R(1)=0 : R(2)=0 : R(3)=0 : R(4)=0 : R(5)=0
1820 FOR I = 6 TO ND
1830   R(I)=(D(I-5)+2*(D(I-4)+D(I-3)+D(I-2))+D(I-1))/8
1840 NEXT I
1850 Q1$="DO YOU WANT TO PRINT THE"
1860 Q2$="DATA  (Y OR N)"
1870 Q3$="" : GOSUB 5000
1880 GOSUB 7800                              'ASK YES OR NO
1890 IF YN$="N" THEN RETURN
1900 CLS
1910 FOR I = 4 TO ND
1920   PRINT R(I),
1930 NEXT I
1940 GOSUB 7400                              'WAIT FOR KEY
1950 RETURN
```

Figure 5.16: Program Listing: Four-Point Centered Average

LINEAR REGRESSION

Description

The linear regression technique allows you to find the "best" straight line for a set of data. The selected line is the one that best meets the regression criteria. You run the Linear Regression program by calling it from the program menu. It uses the data stored with the Input Data program. The program displays the equation for the straight line on your screen. You can also plot the straight line with the plot program, but the resulting plot will not appear straight because of the vertical resolution of the display.

Example

Frank has obtained data from an experiment and would like the equation for the best straight line for these data. The data are:

Point	1	2	3	4	5	6	7	8	9	10	11
Data	1	2	3	5	5	6	7	9	10	11	11
Point	12	13	14	15	16	17	18	19	20	21	22
Data	12	13	14	14	15	16	17	19	20	21	22

The screen display for this example appears in Figure 5.17. The program listing is shown in Figure 5.18.

□□□

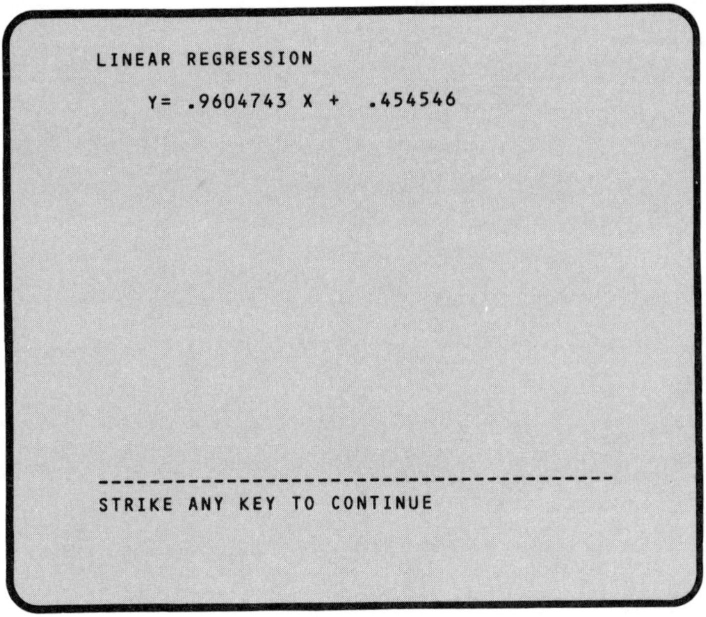

Figure 5.17: Screen Display: Linear Regression

```
1960 REM -----------------------------
1970 N$=      "LINEAR REGRESSION"
1980 REM -----------------------------
1990 GOSUB 6200                           'INITIALIZE
2000 SX=0 : SY=0 : SXY=0 : SX2=0
2010 FOR I = 1 TO ND
2020   SX=SX+I
2030   SY=SY+D(I)
2040   SXY=SXY+D(I)*I
2050   SX2=SX2+I^2
2060 NEXT I
2070 M=(SXY-SX*SY/ND)/(SX2-SX^2/ND)
2080 B=SY/ND-M*SX/ND
2090 PRINT "    Y=";M;"X + " ;B
2100 REM UPDATE RESULT ARRAY
2110 FOR I= 1 TO ND
2120   R(I)=B+M*I
2130 NEXT I
2140 GOSUB 7400
2150 RETURN
```

Figure 5.18: Program Listing: Linear Regression

6

RECORD KEEPING PROGRAMS

This chapter shows you how to use the diskette storage system to store, retrieve, and analyze data. We shall first create a personal file that you can use to store names and addresses. You can use the personal files you create for phone directories, business mailing lists, and other applications. Then we'll show you how to create an automobile file that will make it easy to keep mileage records for your car.

Disk file programs don't usually appear in collections of programs, because they can be very complicated. But by using our central subroutine library, we have been able to reduce the usual complexity of these disk file programs. The results are programs that are easy to enter and use.

Prior to using the programs in this chapter, you must add several new subroutines to the SUBLIB file. These subroutines begin at line numbers 3000, 3800, and 4600; the subroutine listings are in Appendix A.

Unlike the other chapters, the programs in this chapter must be saved in *two* files—one containing the Personal File programs and the other containing the Automobile File programs. Each set of programs begins with a menu.

These programs automatically create data files on disk drive A. You can add these files to your program disk, or you can use a freshly formatted disk.

First let's define a few terms. An *item* is the smallest quantity stored in a file. For the personal file the items are last name, first name, telephone number, street address, city, state, and zip code. The items in the auto record are date, odometer reading, and gallons of gas used. A *record* is defined as a set of items. For the personal file a record is the name, address, and phone number for each individual. Finally, a *file* is a set of records.

PERSONAL FILE MENU

The programs for the personal file run from a menu. As you can see, the individual programs allow you to add a record, delete a record, list the entire file, and search for an individual record in the file. When you begin, you will create your file using the Add Record program. You also add subsequent records with the same program. The Delete Record program removes records from your file; you also change a record by deleting it and then reentering it with new information. The List File program displays the entire file on your screen or printer. The Search Record program allows you to find all records with the same last name. Figure 6.1 shows the menu screen display. Figure 6.2 shows the menu program listing.

□□□

```
1 = ADD RECORD
2 = LIST FILE
3 = DELETE RECORD
4 = SEARCH FILE




-----------------------------------------

CHOOSE PROGRAM :
```

Figure 6.1: Screen Display: Personal File Menu

```
100 REM ------------------------------
110 N$=        "PERSONAL FILE"
120 REM ------------------------------
130 GOSUB 6200                          'INITIALIZE
140 X$(1)="ADD RECORD"
150 X$(2)="LIST FILE"
160 X$(3)="DELETE RECORD"
170 X$(4)="SEARCH FILE"
180 REM DECLARE NO. OF FIELDS AND NAMES
190 F$(1)="LAST NAME"
200 F$(2)="FIRST NAME"
210 F$(3)="TELEPHONE"
220 F$(4)="STREET ADDRESS"
230 F$(5)="CITY"
240 F$(6)="STATE"
250 F$(7)="ZIP"
260 NF=7 : F$="PERS.BAS"  : FB$="PERS.BAK"
270 N=4 : GOSUB 7000                    'DISPLAY MENU
280 ON X GOSUB 690,470,750,830
290 GOTO 100
```

Figure 6.2: Program Listing: Personal File Menu

PERSONAL FILE SUBROUTINES

As you enter the menu program you should also enter the two subroutines shown in Figure 6.3. These routines are used by the List Personal File program to list your files on the screen or on your printer. They handle the formatting differences between the two output devices. The screen program also contains a delay function, which scrolls the screen slowly enough to read the names as they go by.

□□□

```
300 REM ------------------------------
310 REM LIST RECORD ON PRINTER
320 REM ------------------------------
330 LPRINT L;". ",P1$;", ";P2$
340 LPRINT, P3$
350 LPRINT, P4$
360 LPRINT, P5$; ", ";P6$;" " P7$
370 LPRINT
380 RETURN
390 REM ------------------------------
400 REM LIST RECORD ON SCREEN
410 REM ------------------------------
420 PRINT L;". ",P1$;", ";P2$
430 PRINT, P3$
440 PRINT, P4$
450 PRINT, P5$; ", ";P6$;" " P7$
460 PRINT : RETURN
```

Figure 6.3: Program Listing: List Personal File Subroutines

ADD RECORD

Description

The Add Record program is the one you use to create your file, as well as to add records to it. You run the program by displaying the Personal File Menu and depressing the 1 on your keyboard. You enter the last name, first name, telephone number, street address, city, state, and zip code for each record in the file. Records are stored in the order in which they are added.

Example

Figure 6.4 shows a screen display for a typical Add Record dialog. Figure 6.5 shows the Add Record program listing.

□□□

```
ADD RECORD

  LAST NAME                SMITH
  FIRST NAME               JOHN
  TELEPHONE                936-1212
  STREET ADDRESS           123 MAIN
  CITY                     WALNUT CREEK
  STATE                    CA
  ZIP                      94596







----------------------------------------
ADD ANOTHER RECORD ?

YES OR NO
```

Figure 6.4: Screen Display: Add Record

```
690 REM ------------------------------
700 N$=          "ADD RECORD"
710 REM ------------------------------
720 REM CALL ADD RECORD SUBROUTINE
730 GOSUB 3000
740 RETURN
```

Figure 6.5: Program Listing: Add Record

LIST PERSONAL FILE

Description

This program lists your personal file. You run the program by activating the Personal File Menu program and depressing the 2 on your keyboard. The program asks the following question:

```
OUTPUT TO PRINTER
YES OR NO
```

Striking a Y causes the entire personal file to be listed on your printer. Striking an N causes the file to be displayed on your screen. Records will scroll on the screen; a delay function scrolls the screen slowly enough for you to read the records.

Example

Figure 6.6 shows a screen display of a personal file. Note that each record has a record number and that blank lines separate individual records. You will use the record number when you delete records from the file. Figure 6.7 displays the program listing for the List Personal File program.

□□□

```
1 .          SMITH, JOHN
             936-1212
             123 MAIN
             WALNUT CREEK, CA 94596

2 .          SMITH, LISA
             936-1212
             123 MAIN
             WALNUT CREEK, CA 94596

3 .          O'BRIEN, RONALD
             767-9080
             43 PANORAMIC
             BERKELEY, CA 94710




----------------------------------------
STRIKE ANY KEY TO CONTINUE
```

Figure 6.6: Screen Display: List Personal File

```
470 REM ------------------------------
480 N$=            "LIST FILE"
490 REM ------------------------------
500 GOSUB 6200              'INITIALIZE
510 Q1$="OUTPUT TO PRINTER"
520 Q2$="" : Q3$="YES OR NO"
530 GOSUB 5000              'PRINT DIALOG
540 GOSUB 7800              'YESNO
550 CLS
560 OPEN F$ FOR INPUT AS #1
570 L=1
580 IF EOF(1) THEN 660
590 INPUT#1,P1$,P2$,P3$,P4$,P5$,P6$,P7$,P8$
600 IF YN$="Y" THEN GOSUB 300 ELSE GOSUB 400
610 IF YN$="Y" THEN GOTO 640
620 FOR I1= 1 TO 100        'DELAY TO READ ON SCREEN
630 NEXT I1
640 L=L+1
650 GOTO 580
660 PRINT :PRINT : PRINT
670 GOSUB 7400              'PAUSE
680 CLOSE: RETURN
```

Figure 6.7: Program Listing: List Personal File

DELETE RECORD

Description

This program is used to delete old information from your personal file. You can correct information by first deleting it with the Delete Record program and then reentering correct data with the Add Record program. You use this program by indicating the number of the record you wish to delete. All subsequent records are renumbered so that the numbering remains consecutive. You can obtain the record number from the List Personal File program or the Search Personal File program. Figure 6.8 is the Delete Record program listing.

□□□

```
750 REM ------------------------------
760 N$=          "DELETE RECORD"
770 REM ------------------------------
780 GOSUB 4600                          'DELETE RECORD
790 IF L <> -1 THEN GOTO 810
800 LOCATE 19,1 : PRINT "RECORD NOT FOUND"
810 Q2$="DELETE" : GOSUB 3400           'ASK FOR ANOTHER
820 IF YN$="N" THEN RETURN ELSE 780
```

Figure 6.8: Program Listing: Delete Record

SEARCH PERSONAL FILE

Description

The Search Personal File program allows you to find an individual record without listing the entire file. You enter the last name of the individual you are searching for. The first record having the same last name you specify is displayed on your screen. Files containing several individuals with the same last name display one matched record at a time. The program then asks if you would like to search for additional matches. The program tells you if no last name matches are found.

The spelling and capitalization you specify must match exactly the spelling and capitalization in your file. Therefore, you must be consistent in the way you add records to your file. If you enter Smith as the last name in your record and you search for the name SMITH, the program will tell you that no match is found.

Example

Let's search for the record for Ronald O'Brien. The screen display is shown in Figure 6.9. Figure 6.10 is the Search Personal File program listing.

□□□

```
   3 .          O'BRIEN, RONALD
                767-9080
                43 PANORAMIC
                BERKELEY, CA 94710







   ----------------------------------------
   WOULD YOU LIKE TO
   SEARCH
   AGAIN Y OR N ?
```

Figure 6.9: Screen Display: Search Personal File

```
830 REM --------------------------------
840 N$=          "SEARCH FILE"
850 REM --------------------------------
860 GOSUB 6200 : F=0 :L=0
870 Q1$="SEARCH FOR LAST NAME"
880 Q2$="" : Q3$="LAST NAME :"
890 GOSUB 5000
900 INPUT NA$
910 OPEN F$ FOR INPUT AS #1
920 L=L+1 : IF EOF(1) THEN 990
930 INPUT#1,P1$,P2$,P3$,P4$,P5$,P6$,P7$,P8$
940 IF P1$ <> NA$ THEN GOTO 920  'NO MATCH TRY AGAIN
950 F=1                          'SET FOUND FLAG
960 LOCATE 5,1 : CLS : GOSUB 400 'DISPLAY REC ON SCRN
970 GOSUB 7400                   'WAIT FOR KEY
980 GOTO 920                     'LOOK FOR NEXT MATCH
990 REM OUT OF RECORDS
1000 CLOSE
1010 LOCATE 19,1
1020 IF F=0 THEN PRINT "NO MATCHES FOUND"
1030 Q2$="SEARCH" : GOSUB 3400   'ASK FOR ANOTHER
1040 IF YN$="N" THEN RETURN ELSE 830
```

Figure 6.10: Program Listing: Search Personal File

AUTOMOBILE FILE MENU

We will now develop a disk file that keeps mileage records for your automobile. You can use these programs to enter a calendar date, odometer reading, and amount of gasoline purchased. The List Automobile File program computes the average miles per gallon and returns that figure in the listing. You call the Automobile Record programs from a menu program. Figure 6.11 shows the screen display for the Automobile Record menu. Figure 6.12 is the menu program listing.

□□□

```
1 = ADD RECORD
2 = LIST FILE
3 = DELETE RECORD




-----------------------------------------


CHOOSE PROGRAM :
```

Figure 6.11: Screen Display: Automobile Record Menu

```
100 REM ------------------------------
110 N$=      "AUTOMOBILE FILE"
120 REM ------------------------------
130 GOSUB 6200                          'INITIALIZE
140 X$(1)="ADD RECORD"
150 X$(2)="LIST FILE"
160 X$(3)="DELETE RECORD"
170 REM DECLARE NO. OF FIELDS AND NAMES
180 F$(1)="DATE"
190 F$(2)="ODOMETER"
200 F$(3)="GALLONS"
210 NF=3 : F$="CAR.BAS"  : FB$="CAR.BAK"
220 N=3 : GOSUB 7000                    'DISPLAY MENU
230 ON X GOSUB 460,250,520,460
240 GOTO 100
```

Figure 6.12: Program Listing: Automobile Record Menu

ADD RECORD

Description

You use the Add Record program to create your automobile file and to add records to it. You enter the date, odometer reading, and gallons of gasoline purchased. Again, records are stored in the order in which they are added. If you make an error as you create a record, the average miles per gallon may be incorrectly computed. You should check your records carefully immediately after you enter them, because an incorrect record is difficult to correct once you have added other records.

Example

On February 17, 1982, you purchase 14.9 gallons of gas with an odometer reading of 13,523 miles. Figure 6.13 shows the screen display as you add this information to your file. Figure 6.14 is a program listing for the Add Record program.

□□□

```
ADD RECORD

  DATE                         2/17/82
  ODOMETER                     13523
  GALLONS                      14.9









-----------------------------------------
ADD ANOTHER RECORD ?

YES OR NO
```

Figure 6.13: Screen Display: Add Record

```
460 REM ------------------------------
470 N$=          "ADD RECORD"
480 REM ------------------------------
490 REM CALL ADD RECORD SUBROUTINE
500 GOSUB 3000
510 RETURN
```

Figure 6.14: Program Listing: Add Record

LIST AUTOMOBILE FILE

Description

The List Automobile File program lists the contents of your automobile record on your screen. This program also computes and displays the average miles per gallon for each record. The screen will scroll slowly enough for you to read the information.

You can easily monitor your car's performance with this program. A sudden drop in average miles per gallon may indicate a problem with your car.

Example

You would like to view the contents of your automobile log. Figure 6.15 is the screen display for this example. Figure 6.16 is the List Automobile File program listing.

□□□

```
LIST FILE

NO.           DATE          MILES         GAL           AVE
 1            1/31/82       12730         15.6
 2            2/7/82        12925         13.1           14.8855
 3            2/12/82       13210         15.8           18.03798
 4            2/17/82       13523         14.9           21.00671
 5            2/22/82       13801         15.2           18.28948

----------------------------------------
STRIKE ANY KEY TO CONTINUE
```

Figure 6.15: Screen Display: List Automobile File

```
250 REM ------------------------------
260 N$=          "LIST FILE"
270 REM ------------------------------
280 GOSUB 6200                 'INITIALIZE
290 MI=0 : GAL=0
300 PRINT "NO.","DATE","MILES","GAL","AVE"
310 OPEN F$ FOR INPUT AS #1
320 L=1
330 IF EOF(1) THEN 440
340 INPUT#1,P1$,P2$,P3$,P4$,P5$,P6$,P7$,P8$
350 GAL =VAL(P3$)
360 AVE=(VAL(P2$)-MI)/GAL
370 MI=VAL(P2$)
380 PRINT L,P1$,P2$,P3$,
390 IF L=1 THEN PRINT ELSE PRINT AVE
400 FOR I1= 1 TO 100           'DELAY TO READ ON SCREEN
410 NEXT I1
420 L=L+1
430 GOTO 330
440 GOSUB 7400                 'PAUSE
450 CLOSE: RETURN
```

Figure 6.16: Program Listing: List Automobile File

DELETE RECORD

Description

The Delete Record program allows you to delete a record from your file. You can use this program to delete information that you enter incorrectly. You delete a record by specifying its number. When you delete a record in the middle of a file, all subsequent records are renumbered so that there are no holes in the file. Figure 6.17 shows the Delete Record program listing. You must delete records immediately upon incorrect entry; otherwise, the program will incorrectly compute miles per gallon.

□□□

```
520 REM ------------------------------
530 N$=        "DELETE RECORD"
540 REM ------------------------------
550 GOSUB 4600                        'DELETE RECORD
560 IF L <> -1 THEN GOTO 580
570 LOCATE 19,1 : PRINT "RECORD NOT FOUND"
580 Q2$="DELETE" : GOSUB 3400         'ASK FOR ANOTHER
590 IF YN$="N" THEN RETURN ELSE 550
```

Figure 6.17: Program Listing: Delete Record

□□□□□□□ 7

MATHEMATICS PRACTICE PROGRAMS

This chapter presents three sets of programs that allow you to use your computer to practice arithmetic. You must save each set in its own file. Each set runs from a menu, which you enter first. We provide drills in addition, subtraction, multiplication, and division, with both whole numbers and fractions. The three menus provide programs at multiple levels of difficulty; the programs are suitable for students from elementary to high school level. All programs keep track of right and wrong answers. You will be greeted with a beep when you answer incorrectly. You will find that these programs can greatly sharpen your math skills; they are also helpful in completing homework assignments!

MATHEMATICS PRACTICE I MENU

The first set of four programs provides practice in adding, subtracting, multiplying, and dividing two whole numbers. You begin this set of programs by displaying the Mathematics Practice I Menu. Depress a number key to choose the drill you want. Once you have chosen the drill, the program asks you to choose the largest number you want to work with. Then the program presents you with two numbers and an operator to indicate addition, subtraction, multiplication, or division. You enter your answer from left to right. The programs generate a beep when you answer incorrectly. Each program keeps track of the total number of correct and incorrect answers. (Be sure to challenge yourself by choosing a large number!)

To use these programs you first enter the menu program and two common subroutines. Figure 7.1 shows the screen display for the menu program. Figure 7.2 is the program listing of the menu program.

□□□

```
1 = ADDITION
2 = SUBTRACTION
3 = MULTIPLICATION
4 = DIVISION







----------------------------------------

CHOOSE PROGRAM :
```

Figure 7.1: Screen Display: Mathematics Practice I Menu

```
100 REM ------------------------------
110 N$=     "MATHEMATICS PRACTICE I"
120 REM ------------------------------
130 GOSUB 6200                          'INITIALIZE
140 K=1                                 'SET INDEX
150 X$(1)="ADDITION"
160 X$(2)="SUBTRACTION"
170 X$(3)="MULTIPLICATION"
180 X$(4)="DIVISION"
190 N=4 : GOSUB 7000
200 R=0 : W=0
210 Q1$="WHAT IS LARGEST NUMBER"
220 Q2$="YOU WOULD LIKE TO"
230 Q3$="PRACTICE WITH"
240 GOSUB 5000                          'ASK QUESTIONS
250 PRINT TAB(20) : INPUT Y
260 ON X GOSUB 500,620,770,890
270 GOTO 100
```

Figure 7.2: Program Listing: Mathematics Practice I Menu

MATHEMATICS PRACTICE I SUBROUTINES

The Mathematics Practice I programs use two subroutines to display the questions and print and tabulate the answers. You must enter them before you enter the actual drills. We use these subroutines to greatly shorten the programs that follow. The subroutines generate problems with a random number generator, keep track of the total problems done and the total number of correct and incorrect answers, and generate the sound. The subroutines are listed in Figure 7.3.

□□□

```
280 REM ------------------------------
290 REM DISPLAY QUESTION AND GET ANSWER
300 REM ------------------------------
310 LOCATE 5,20 :PRINT USING "####";N1
320 LOCATE 6,19 :PRINT SN$; : PRINT USING "####";N2
330 LOCATE  7,20 :PRINT"----"
340 PRINT "TYPE ANSWER        ";
350 INPUT A
360 PRINT "CORRECT ANSWER IS :" ;
370 RETURN
380 REM ------------------------------
390 REM FINISH THE PROBLEM
400 REM ------------------------------
410 PRINT :PRINT "YOU ARE ";
420 IF S=1 THEN PRINT "RIGHT" ELSE PRINT "WRONG"
430 IF S=1 THEN R=R+1 ELSE W=W+1      'UPDATE SCORE
440 IF S=0 THEN SOUND 500,9           'BOO FOR WRONG
450 PRINT "PROBLEMS DONE";TAB(20);R+W
460 PRINT "CORRECT";TAB(20);R
470 PRINT "ERRORS";TAB(20);W
480 Q2$="PRACTICE" : GOSUB 3400       'ASK FOR ANOTHER
490 RETURN
```

Figure 7.3: Program Listing: Mathematics Practice I Subroutines

ADDITION

Description

The addition drill presents two random numbers at a time. You must enter the answer from left to right, which will sometimes mean that you must first work out the problem on a piece of paper. The program selects the largest number you work with from the answer you enter when the menu first appears.

Example

The sample display in Figure 7.4 shows the incorrect addition of the numbers 20 and 14. Note that six problems have been done; four out of six answers have been correct. The Addition program is listed in Figure 7.5.

□□□

```
ADDITION DRILL


                        20
                    +   14
                      ----
TYPE ANSWER         ? 6
CORRECT ANSWER IS :   34

YOU ARE WRONG
PROBLEMS DONE         6
CORRECT               4
ERRORS                2





----------------------------------------
WOULD YOU LIKE TO
PRACTICE
AGAIN Y OR N ?
```

Figure 7.4: Screen Display: Addition

```
500 REM ------------------------------
510 N$=       "ADDITION DRILL"
520 REM ------------------------------
530 GOSUB 6200
540 N1=INT(RND(Y)*Y)
550 N2=INT(RND(Y)*Y)
560 SN$="+"
570 GOSUB 280                          'DISP QUEST,GET ANS
580 IF A=N1+N2 THEN S=1 ELSE S=0       'SET FLAG
590 PRINT USING "####"; N1+N2
600 GOSUB 380                          'FINISH UP
610 IF YN$="N" THEN RETURN ELSE 530
```

Figure 7.5: Program Listing: Addition

SUBTRACTION

Description

The subtraction drill is similar to the addition drill. The program's selection method for the two numbers guarantees that a positive answer always results. Remember, practice makes perfect—try lots of problems.

Example

The screen display in Figure 7.6 shows the incorrect subtraction of 4 from 31. Note that two out of three problems have been correctly answered. Figure 7.7 displays the program listing for the subtraction drill.

□□□

```
SUBTRACTION DRILL



                          31
                      -    4
                        ----
TYPE ANSWER           ? 6
CORRECT ANSWER IS :     27

YOU ARE WRONG
PROBLEMS DONE           3
CORRECT                 2
ERRORS                  1




-------------------------------------------
WOULD YOU LIKE TO
PRACTICE
AGAIN Y OR N ?
```

Figure 7.6: Screen Display: Subtraction

```
620 REM ------------------------------
630 N$=      "SUBTRACTION DRILL"
640 REM ------------------------------
650 GOSUB 6200
660 N1=INT(RND(Y)*Y)
670 N2=INT(RND(Y)*Y)
680 N3=N1
690 IF N1 > N2 GOTO 710
700 N1=N2  :  N2=N3
710 SN$="-"
720 GOSUB 280                      'DISP QUEST,GET ANS
730 IF A=N1-N2 THEN S=1 ELSE S=0   'SET FLAG
740 PRINT USING "####"; N1-N2
750 GOSUB 380                      'FINISH UP
760 IF YN$="N" THEN RETURN ELSE 620
```

Figure 7.7: Program Listing: Subtraction

MULTIPLICATION

Description

This program allows you to practice multiplying two numbers. The program generates random numbers; you choose the largest number you want to work with at the time you select the multiplication drill from the menu. This program displays the answer on a single line. If you are multiplying by two or more digits, you may wish to use the Long Multiplication program that appears later in this chapter. The Long Multiplication program displays the intermediate steps necessary to compute the answer.

Example

Figure 7.8 shows the screen display for the multiplication of 0 times 7. The display shows that four out of five problems have been correctly done. Figure 7.9 is the program listing for the multiplication drill.

□□□

```
MULTIPLICATION DRILL


                         0
                     X   7
                      ----
TYPE ANSWER          ? 0
CORRECT ANSWER IS :      0

YOU ARE RIGHT
PROBLEMS DONE          5
CORRECT                4
ERRORS                 1




----------------------------------------
WOULD YOU LIKE TO
PRACTICE
AGAIN Y OR N ?
```

Figure 7.8: Screen Display: Multiplication

```
770 REM ------------------------------
780 N$=     "MULTIPLICATION DRILL"
790 REM ------------------------------
800 GOSUB 6200
810 N1=INT(RND(Y)*Y)
820 N2=INT(RND(Y)*Y)
830 SN$="X"
840 GOSUB 280                        'DISP QUEST,GET ANS
850 IF A=N1*N2 THEN S=1 ELSE S=0     'SET FLAG
860 PRINT USING "####"; N1*N2
870 GOSUB 380                        'FINISH UP
880 IF YN$="N" THEN RETURN ELSE 770
```

Figure 7.9: Program Listing: Multiplication

DIVISION

Description

The fourth mathematics drill allows you to practice dividing two whole numbers. Again, you choose the largest number you want to divide by (the denominator) when the Division program is selected from the Mathematics Practice I Menu. The program generates numbers which guarantee that a whole number results from your division. Note that the largest number you work with is the largest answer in this program.

Example

Figure 7.10 displays a division of 80 by 16. Note that this is the fifth problem completed, and that all the answers have been correct. The listing for the Division program appears in Figure 7.11.

□□□

```
DIVISION DRILL



                    80
                 /  16
                  ----
TYPE ANSWER      ? 5
CORRECT ANSWER IS :   5

YOU ARE RIGHT
PROBLEMS DONE       5
CORRECT             5
ERRORS              0





----------------------------------------
WOULD YOU LIKE TO
PRACTICE
AGAIN Y OR N ?
```

Figure 7.10: Screen Display: Division

```
890 REM ------------------------------
900 N$=        "DIVISION DRILL"
910 REM ------------------------------
920 GOSUB 6200
930 N1=INT(RND(Y)*Y)
940 N2=INT(RND(Y)*Y)  : IF N2=0 THEN 940
950 N1=N1*N2
960 SN$="/"
970 GOSUB 280                        'DISP QUEST,GET ANS
980 IF A=N1/N2 THEN S=1 ELSE S=0     'SET FLAG
990 PRINT USING "####"; N1/N2
1000 GOSUB 380                       'FINISH UP
1010 IF YN$="N" THEN RETURN ELSE 890
```

Figure 7.11: Program Listing: Division

MATHEMATICS PRACTICE II MENU

Mathematics Practice II consists of two advanced mathematics drills. The first program allows you to practice adding numbers in columns. The second program allows you to practice multiplying large numbers using long multiplication. For both programs, work out the answer with pencil and paper and then enter it into the computer. Note that the multiplication program provides all intermediate steps. Figure 7.12 is a screen display of the Mathematics Practice II menu. Figure 7.13 is a listing of the menu program.

□□□

```
1 = COLUMN ADDITION
2 = LONG MULTIPLICATION




----------------------------------------

CHOOSE PROGRAM :
```

Figure 7.12: Screen Display: Mathematics Practice II Menu

```
100 REM ------------------------------
110 N$=   "MATHEMATICS PRACTICE II"
120 REM ------------------------------
130 GOSUB 6200                          'INITIALIZE
140 K=1                                 'SET INDEX
150 X$(1)="COLUMN ADDITION"
160 X$(2)="LONG MULTIPLICATION"
170 REM SET UP MENU AND DISPLAY IT
180 N=2 : GOSUB 7000                    'DISPLAY MENU
190 ON X GOSUB 210,580                  'SELECT PROGRAM
200 GOTO 100
```

Figure 7.13: Program Listing: Mathematics Practice II Menu

COLUMN ADDITION

Description

The Column Addition program allows you to practice adding columns of numbers. You select this drill by depressing the number 1 from the menu program. The program then asks you to enter both the largest number and how many numbers you would like to add. The program keeps track of correct and incorrect answers.

Example

Figure 7.14 shows the correct addition of the five numbers 15, 4, 15, 21, and 18. Figure 7.15 is the program listing for this mathematics drill.

```
210 REM ------------------------------
220 N$=     "COLUMN ADDITION"
230 REM ------------------------------
240 GOSUB 6200                              'INITIALIZE
250 Q1$=""
260 Q2$="WHAT IS LARGEST NUMBER"
270 Q3$="YOU WOULD LIKE TO ADD"
280 GOSUB 5000
290 INPUT LG                                'GET NUMBER
300 Q2$="HOW MANY NUMBERS"
310 GOSUB 5000
320 INPUT NU
330 R=0 :W=0
340 GOSUB 6200                              'INITIALIZE
350 TOT=0
```

Figure 7.15: Program Listing: Column Addition (continues)

```
COLUMN ADDITION

                          15
                           4
                          15
                          21
                          18
                      ------
YOUR ANSWER          ? 73

CORRECT ANSWER            73
YOU ARE RIGHT
PROBLEMS DONE        1
CORRECT              1
WRONG                0



----------------------------------------
WOULD YOU LIKE TO
ADD
AGAIN Y OR N ?
```

Figure 7.14: Screen Display: Column Addition

```
360 FOR I=1 TO NU
370     N1=INT(RND(LG)*LG)
380     TOT=TOT+N1
390     PRINT TAB(20);
400     PRINT USING "######";N1
410 NEXT I
420 PRINT TAB(20) ;"------"
430 PRINT "YOUR ANSWER";TAB(20);
440 INPUT A
450 PRINT
460 PRINT "CORRECT ANSWER"; TAB(20)
470 PRINT USING "######";TOT
480 IF TOT=A THEN S=1 ELSE S=0
490 PRINT "YOU ARE ";
500 IF S=1 THEN R=R+1 ELSE W=W+1
510 IF S=1 THEN PRINT "RIGHT" ELSE PRINT "WRONG"
520 IF S=0 THEN SOUND 500,9          'ADD SOME SOUND
530 PRINT "PROBLEMS DONE";TAB(20);R+W
540 PRINT "CORRECT";TAB(20);R
550 PRINT"WRONG";TAB(20);W
560 Q2$="ADD" : GOSUB 3400           'ASK FOR ANOTHER
570 IF YN$="N" THEN RETURN ELSE 340
```

Figure 7.15: Program Listing: Column Addition

LONG MULTIPLICATION

Description

We now present a program that allows you to practice multiplying numbers using long multiplication. You select this program from the Mathematics Practice II Menu by pressing the 2 on your keyboard. You then enter the number of digits you wish to work with. The program presents you with two numbers to multiply; you work out your answer by hand and enter the final answer. The screen displays the correct answer and the steps that are necessary to compute the answer. By reviewing the various steps, you can see exactly where you make your mistakes.

Example

Figure 7.16 shows the result of multiplying 4198 by 8610. Note that all of the intermediate results are displayed. Figure 7.17 is the Long Multiplication program listing.

```
580 REM -----------------------------
590 N$=      "LONG MULTIPLICATION"
600 REM -----------------------------
610 GOSUB 6200                            'INITIALIZE
620 Q1$=""
630 Q2$="HOW MANY DIGITS"
640 Q3$="YOU WOULD LIKE TO MULTIPLY"
650 GOSUB 5000                            'GET NUMBER
660 INPUT N
670 GOSUB 6200
680 N1=0 : N2=0
690 FOR I=0 TO N-1
700    N1(I)=INT(RND(N)*10) : N1=N1+N1(I)*10^I
710    N2(I)=INT(RND(N)*10) : N2=N2+N2(I)*10^I
720 NEXT I
```

Figure 7.17: Program Listing: Long Multiplication (continues)

```
LONG MULTIPLICATION

                              4198
                              8610
                        ----------
                                 0
                             41980
                           2518800
                          33584000
                        __________
                          36144780




TYPE YOUR ANSWER    ->? 36144780

YOU ARE RIGHT

----------------------------------------
WOULD YOU LIKE TO
MULTIPLY
AGAIN Y OR N ?
```

Figure 7.16: Screen Display: Long Multiplication

```
730 PRINT TAB(20) : PRINT USING "##########" ; N1
740 PRINT TAB(20) : PRINT USING "##########" ; N2
750 PRINT TAB(20);"----------"
760 LOCATE 16,1
770 PRINT "TYPE YOUR ANSWER   ->";
780 INPUT A
790 LOCATE 6,1
800 FOR I= 0 TO N-1
810    PRINT TAB(20)
815    PRINT USING "##########"; N1*N2(I)*10^I
820 NEXT I
830 PRINT TAB(20);"__________"
840 PRINT TAB(20): PRINT USING "##########"; N1*N2
845 PRINT
850 LOCATE 18,1 : PRINT "YOU ARE ";
860 IF N1*N2=A THEN S=1 ELSE S=0
870 IF S=1 THEN PRINT "RIGHT" ELSE PRINT "WRONG"
880 IF S=0 THEN SOUND 500,9          'SOUND OFF
890 Q2$="MULTIPLY" : GOSUB 3400
900 IF YN$="N" THEN RETURN ELSE 670
```

Figure 7.17: Program Listing: Long Multiplication

MATHEMATICS PRACTICE III MENU

The final set of mathematics drills allows you to practice adding, subtracting, multiplying, and dividing fractions. You work out your answers by hand and enter the final answer. All answers in this section are reduced to least-common-denominator form; conversions to mixed numbers are not made. Each program keeps track of your correct and incorrect answers.

The four fraction programs work from a common menu. Figure 7.18 displays the Mathematics Practice III Menu; Figure 7.19 is the listing of the menu program.

□□□

```
1 = ADDITION
2 = SUBTRACTION
3 = MULTIPLICATION
4 = DIVISION




----------------------------------------

CHOOSE PROGRAM :
```

Figure 7.18: Screen Display: Mathematics Practice III Menu

```
100 REM ------------------------------
110 N$=   "MATHEMATICS PRACTICE III"
120 REM ------------------------------
130 DEFINT D-N
140 GOSUB 6200                          'INITIALIZE
150 K=1                                 'SET INDEX
160 X$(1)="ADDITION"
170 X$(2)="SUBTRACTION"
180 X$(3)="MULTIPLICATION"
190 X$(4)="DIVISION"
200 N=4 : GOSUB 7000
210 R=0 : W=0
220 Q1$="WHAT IS LARGEST DENOMINATOR"
230 Q2$="YOU WOULD LIKE TO"
240 Q3$="PRACTICE WITH"
250 GOSUB 5000                          'ASK QUESTIONS
260 PRINT TAB(20) : INPUT Y
270 ON X GOSUB 810,950,1100,1240
280 GOTO 100
```

Figure 7.19: Program Listing: Mathematics Practice III Menu

FRACTION SUBROUTINES

Prior to entering the fraction program, you should enter the four subroutines shown in Figure 7.20. These subroutines generate the fractions and the greatest common denominator, display the question, and print the answer.

The subroutines use a random number generator to select the numerators and denominators. They also display the problem on the screen in fraction form, as shown below:

```
 4   5
 — + —
 5   6
```

When you answer, the subroutines ask you for the numerator and denominator separately.

□□□

```
290 REM ------------------------------------------------
300 REM ROUTINE TO GENERATE NUMERATORS AND DENOMINATORS
310 REM ------------------------------------------------
320 DEF FNND(Y)=INT(RND(Y)*Y)  'GEN TRIAL NUM OR DENOM
330 N1=FNND(Y) : IF N1=0 THEN 330
340 N2=FNND(Y) : IF N2=0 THEN 340
350 D1=FNND(Y) : IF D1=0 THEN 350
360 D2=FNND(Y) : IF D2=0 THEN 360
370 IF N1/D1 >= N2/D2 THEN 400 'ENSURE SUBT IS POSITIVE
380 N3=N2 : N2=N1 : N1=N3      'OTHERWISE SWAP
390 D3=D2 : D2=D1 : D1=D3
400 RETURN
410 REM --------------------------------------------
420 REM ROUTINE TO FIND GREATEST COMMON DENOMINATOR
430 REM --------------------------------------------
440 U=N3 : V=D3
450 G=U-V*INT(U/V)
460 IF G=0 THEN RETURN
470 U=V
480 V=G
490 GOTO 450
500 REM ------------------------------
510 REM DISPLAY QUESTION AND GET ANSWER
520 REM ------------------------------
530 LOCATE 5,20
540 PRINT USING "###   ";N1;N2
550 LOCATE 6,20
560 PRINT "--- ";SN$;" ---"
570 LOCATE 7,20
580 PRINT USING "###   ";D1;D2
590 PRINT "TYPE NUMERATOR    ";
600 INPUT AN                     'INPUT ANSWER
610 PRINT "TYPE DENOMINATOR  ";
620 INPUT AD
630 PRINT : PRINT "CORRECT ANSWER IS :"
640 RETURN
650 REM -------------------------
660 REM FINISH THE PROBLEM
670 REM -------------------------
680 PRINT TAB(20); : PRINT USING "###" ; N3
690 PRINT TAB(20);"---"
700 PRINT  TAB(20); : PRINT USING "###";D3
710 IF AN=N3 AND AD=D3 THEN S=1 ELSE S=0
720 PRINT :PRINT "YOU ARE ";
730 IF S=1 THEN PRINT "RIGHT" ELSE PRINT "WRONG"
740 IF S=1 THEN R=R+1 ELSE W=W+1  'UPDATE SCORE
750 IF S=0 THEN SOUND 500,9       'BOO FOR WRONG
760 PRINT "PROBLEMS DONE";TAB(20);R+W
770 PRINT "CORRECT";TAB(20);R
780 PRINT "ERRORS";TAB(20);W
790 Q2$="PRACTICE " : GOSUB 3400  'ASK FOR ANOTHER
800 RETURN
```

Figure 7.20: Program Listing: Fraction Subroutines

FRACTION ADDITION

Description

The Fraction Addition drill allows you to practice adding two fractions. You select this program from the fraction program menu by striking the 1 on your keyboard. You must also enter the largest denominator you want to work with. (Don't be afraid of large denominators!)

Example

Figure 7.21 shows the result of the addition 2/1 + 1/2. Note that this is the second problem of a series. Figure 7.22 is the program listing for the addition drill.

□□□

```
ADDITION DRILL



                          2      1
                         --- + ---
                          1      2
TYPE NUMERATOR     ? 5
TYPE DENOMINATOR   ? 2

CORRECT ANSWER IS :
                          5
                         ---
                          2

YOU ARE RIGHT
PROBLEMS DONE            2
CORRECT                  1
ERRORS                   1
------------------------------------------
WOULD YOU LIKE TO
PRACTICE
AGAIN Y OR N ?
```

Figure 7.21: Screen Display: Fraction Addition

```
810 REM ------------------------------
820 N$=        "ADDITION DRILL"
830 REM ------------------------------
840 GOSUB 6200
850 GOSUB 290              'GENERATE NUMS AND DENOMS
860 SN$="+"
870 GOSUB 500              'DISP QUEST,GET ANS
880 N3=D2*N1 +D1*N2        'BEFORE CLEANUP
890 D3=D1*D2
900 REM FIND GREATEST COMMON DENOM
910 GOSUB 410
920 N3=N3/V  : D3=D3/V
930 GOSUB 650              'FINISH UP
940 IF YN$="N" THEN RETURN ELSE 840
```

Figure 7.22: Program Listing: Fraction Addition

FRACTION SUBTRACTION

Description

You can practice subtracting fractions with this program. You select the program by pressing 2 as you run the fraction drill menu. You also select the largest denominator you want to work with. Like the subtraction drill in the first menu, this program generates its numbers so that a positive answer always results.

Example

Figure 7.23 shows the result of the operation 2/2 – 1/2. Figure 7.24 is the program listing for the Fraction Subtraction program.

□□□

```
SUBTRACTION DRILL



                      2      1
                     --- - ---
                      2      2
TYPE NUMERATOR    ? 1
TYPE DENOMINATOR  ? 2

CORRECT ANSWER IS :
                      1
                     ---
                      2


YOU ARE RIGHT
PROBLEMS DONE         1
CORRECT               1
ERRORS                0
----------------------------------------
WOULD YOU LIKE TO
PRACTICE
AGAIN Y OR N ?
```

Figure 7.23: Screen Display: Fraction Subtraction

```
950 REM ------------------------------
960 N$=      "SUBTRACTION DRILL"
970 REM ------------------------------
980 GOSUB 6200
990 GOSUB 290                'GENERATE NUMS AND DENOMS
1000 N3=D2*N1 -D1*N2         'BEFORE CLEANUP
1010 IF N3=0 THEN 990        'DISALLOW 0
1020 SN$="-"
1030 GOSUB 500               'DISP QUEST,GET ANS
1040 D3=D1*D2
1050 REM FIND GREATEST COMMON DENOM
1060 GOSUB 410
1070 N3=N3/V  : D3=D3/V
1080 GOSUB 650               'FINISH UP
1090 IF YN$="N" THEN RETURN ELSE 950
```

Figure 7.24: Program Listing: Fraction Subtraction

FRACTION MULTIPLICATION

Description

The Fraction Multiplication program allows you to practice multiplying two fractions. You select this program from the fraction menu by pressing the number 3. Fraction multiplication is very easy to learn, and it comes in handy—don't be afraid to try this drill.

Example

Figure 7.25 shows the result of multiplying the fractions 2/1 × 1/2. Note that two out of four problems have been correctly answered. Figure 7.26 is the Fraction Multiplication program listing.

□□□

```
MULTIPLICATION DRILL


                          2     1
                         --- X ---
                          1     2
TYPE NUMERATOR       ? 1
TYPE DENOMINATOR     ? 1

CORRECT ANSWER IS :
                          1
                         ---
                          1


YOU ARE RIGHT
PROBLEMS DONE            4
CORRECT                  2
ERRORS                   2
---------------------------------------
WOULD YOU LIKE TO
PRACTICE
AGAIN Y OR N ?
```

Figure 7.25: Screen Display: Fraction Multiplication

```
1100 REM ------------------------------
1110 N$=      "MULTIPLICATION DRILL"
1120 REM ------------------------------
1130 GOSUB 6200
1140 GOSUB 290                'GENERATE NUMS AND DENOMS
1150 SN$="X"
1160 GOSUB 500                'DISP QUEST,GET ANS
1170 N3=N1*N2                 'BEFORE CLEANUP
1180 D3=D1*D2
1190 REM FIND GREATEST COMMON DENOM
1200 GOSUB 410
1210 N3=N3/V  : D3=D3/V
1220 GOSUB 650                'FINISH UP
1230 IF YN$="N" THEN RETURN ELSE 1100
```

Figure 7.26: Program Listing: Fraction Multiplication

FRACTION DIVISION

Description

The final fraction program allows you to practice dividing fractions. This program is chosen by pressing the 4 on your keyboard from the menu program. Dividing fractions is the same as multiplying fractions, except that you invert the second fraction (the denominator). Practice with this program will sharpen your skills and make fraction division a less formidable task for you.

Example

Figure 7.27 shows a screen display for the problem (3/1)/(3/2). Figure 7.28 lists the Fraction Division program.

□□□

```
DIVISION DRILL



                         3      3
                        --- / ---
                         1      2
TYPE NUMERATOR     ? 2
TYPE DENOMINATOR   ? 1

CORRECT ANSWER IS :
                         2
                        ---
                         1


YOU ARE RIGHT
PROBLEMS DONE          1
CORRECT                1
ERRORS                 0
----------------------------------------
WOULD YOU LIKE TO
PRACTICE
AGAIN Y OR N ?
```

Figure 7.27: Screen Display: Fraction Division

```
1240 REM ------------------------------
1250 N$=       "DIVISION DRILL"
1260 REM ------------------------------
1270 GOSUB 6200
1280 GOSUB 290               'GENERATE NUMS AND DENOMS
1290 N3=N1*D2                'BEFORE CLEANUP
1300 D3=D1*N2
1310 REM FIND GREATEST COMMON DENOM
1320 GOSUB 410
1330 N3=N3/V  : D3=D3/V
1340 SN$="/"
1350 GOSUB 500               'DISP QUEST,GET ANS
1360 GOSUB 650               'FINISH UP
1370 IF YN$="N" THEN RETURN ELSE 1240
1380 PRINT YN$  :  RETURN
```

Figure 7.28: Program Listing: Fraction Division

□□□ APPENDIX A

CENTRAL SUBROUTINES

The concept of central subroutines is unique to this book. These subroutines allow us to create useful programs that are very short and thus easy to enter. Interested users should read Appendix B to see how these subroutines can be used in other applications.

This appendix contains the program listings for the central subroutines used throughout the book. The programs contain many remark statements to help you understand the functions of each subroutine.

You can save retyping these subroutines many times by saving them together in one disk file. (Remember to save them in ASCII format by using the ,A option.) Add them to your application programs with the MERGE command, as explained in Chapter 1. Remember that you need type only the first REM in each subroutine.

```
3000 REM           "ADREC"
3001 ' ------------------------------
3002 '      ADD RECORDS TO FILE
3003 '
3004 'THIS ROUTINE ADDS RECORDS TO A FILE
3005 '
3006 'CALLING PARAMETERS:
3007 '     NF= NUMBER OF FIELDS IN RECORD (MAX=8)
3008 '     F$(L)=NAMES OF FIELDS
3009 '     F$=NAME OF FILE TO ADD TO
3010 '
3011 'RETURNED PARAMETERS:
3012 '     NONE
3013 '
3014 'COMMENT: ADDS RECORDS TILL TERMINATED BY USER
3015 '        8 FIELDS ARE CREATED EVEN IF BLANK
3016 '
3017 ' ------------------------------
3020 OPEN F$ FOR APPEND AS #1
3030 K=1  : GOSUB 6200                'INITIALIZE
3040 Q1$="ENTER DATA"
3050 Q2$=""
3060 FOR L= 1 TO NF
3070   Q3$=F$(L) : GOSUB 5800         'ASK FOR DATA
3080 NEXT L
3090 WRITE#1,P$(1),P$(2),P$(3),P$(4),P$(5),P$(6),P$(7),P$(8)
3100 REM SEE IF MORE RECORDS TO BE ADDED
3110 Q1$="ADD ANOTHER RECORD ? "
3120 Q2$="" : Q3$="YES OR NO"
3130 GOSUB 5000                       'PRESENT DIALOG
3140 GOSUB 7800                       'YESNO
3150 IF YN$="Y" GOTO 3030
3160 CLOSE : RETURN
```

Figure A.1: Add Record Subroutine

```
3400 REM          "ANOTH"
3401 ' -------------------------------
3402 '      ASK FOR ANOTHER RUN
3403 '
3404 'THIS ROUTINE ASKS THE USER WHETHER TO CONTINUE
3405 '
3406 'CALLING PARAMETERS:
3407 '     Q2$= STRING TO SPECIFY WHAT OPERATION TO DO
3408 '
3409 'RETURNED PARAMETERS:
3410 '     YN$= A "Y" OR "N" FOR YES OR NO
3411 '
3412 ' -------------------------------
3420 Q1$="WOULD YOU LIKE TO "
3430 Q3$="AGAIN Y OR N ?"
3440 GOSUB 5000                           'PRESENT DIALOG
3450 GOSUB 7800                           'ASK YES OR NO
3460 RETURN
```

Figure A.2: Request to Run Again Subroutine

```
3800 REM          "BAKFIL"
3801 ' -------------------------------
3802 '      BACK UP A FILE
3803 '
3804 'THIS ROUTINE CREATES A BACKUP COPY OF A FILE
3805 '
3806 'CALLING PARAMETERS:
3807 '     F$= NAME OF FILE TO BACKUP
3808 '     FB$=NAME OF BACKUP FILE
3809 '
3810 ' -------------------------------
3820 OPEN F$ FOR INPUT AS #1
3830 OPEN FB$ FOR OUTPUT AS #2
3840 'READ A RECORD, THEN WRITE IT
3850 FOR I= 1 TO 4000
3860   IF EOF(1) THEN GOTO 3900      'TILL END OF FILE
3870   INPUT#1,P1$,P2$,P3$,P4$,P5$,P6$,P7$,P8$
3880   WRITE#2,P1$,P2$,P3$,P4$,P5$,P6$,P7$,P8$
3890 NEXT I
3900 CLOSE
3910 RETURN
```

Figure A.3: Create Backup File Subroutine

```
4600 REM           "DELREC"
4601 ' --------------------------------
4602 '     DELETE RECORD
4603 '
4604 'THIS ROUTINE DELETES A RECORD FROM A FILE
4605 '
4606 'CALLING PARAMETERS:
4607 '    FB$= NAME OF BACKUP FILE TO CREATE
4608 '    F$=NAME OF FILE TO DELETE FROM
4609 '
4610 'RETURNED PARAMETERS:
4611 '    L=-1 IF RECORD NOT FOUND
4612 '
4613 'COMMENT-USER IS ASKED FOR RECORD NUMBER
4614 '          BACKUP FILE IS CREATED
4615 '
4616 ' --------------------------------
4620 N$="DELETE RECORD" : GOSUB 6200    'INITIALIZE
4630 Q1$="NUMBER OF RECORD TO DELETE"
4640 Q2$="" : Q3$=""
4650 GOSUB 5000                         'ASK QUESTION
4660 INPUT L                            'GET REC NUMBER
4670 GOSUB 3800                         'CREATE BACKUP
4680 OPEN FB$ FOR INPUT AS #1
4690 OPEN F$ FOR OUTPUT AS #2
4700 FOR I = 1 TO L-1
4710   IF EOF(1) THEN  GOTO 4860        'REC NOT FOUND
4720   INPUT#1,P1$,P2$,P3$,P4$,P5$,P6$,P7$,P8$
4730   WRITE#2,P1$,P2$,P3$,P4$,P5$,P6$,P7$,P8$
4740 NEXT I
4750 REM READ BUT DON'T WRITE RECORD TO DELETE
4760   INPUT#1,P1$,P2$,P3$,P4$,P5$,P6$,P7$,P8$
4770 REM READ AND WRITE TILL END OF FILE
4780 FOR I= 1 TO 4000
4790   IF EOF(1) THEN GOTO 4840
4800   INPUT#1,P1$,P2$,P3$,P4$,P5$,P6$,P7$,P8$
4810   WRITE#2,P1$,P2$,P3$,P4$,P5$,P6$,P7$,P8$
4820 NEXT I
4830 REM NORMAL RETURN
4840 CLOSE  : RETURN
4850 REM ERROR RETURN
4860 CLOSE
4870 L=-1                               'SET ERROR FLAG
4880 RETURN
```

Figure A.4: Delete Record Subroutine

```
5000 REM       "DIALOG"
5001 ' -------------------------------
5002 '        DIALOGUE
5003 '
5004 'CALLING PARAMETERS:
5005 '    Q1$,Q2$,Q3$, = QUESTIONS TO DISPLAY
5006 '
5007 'RETURNED PARAMETERS:
5008 '    NONE
5009 '
5010 'COMMENT: UNUSED QUESTION STRINGS SHOULD BE SET
5011 '          TO NULL ( "" )
5012 '
5013 ' -------------------------------
5020 FOR I= 20 TO 23
5030  LOCATE I,1
5040  IF I > 20 THEN 5080
5050    FOR J= 1 TO 40            'DRAW A BORDER
5060      PRINT "-";
5070    NEXT J
5080  IF I = 21 THEN PRINT Q1$; 'FIRST QUESTION
5090  IF I = 22 THEN PRINT Q2$; 'SECOND QUESTION
5100  IF I = 23 THEN PRINT Q3$; 'THIRD QUESTION
5109 REM RESTORE CURSOR HERE AFTER 3RD QUEST
5110  CP1=POS(N)
5120  CP=POS(N)                  'CURSOR COLUMN POSITION
5130  IF CP>40 THEN 5150
5140   PRINT " "; : GOTO 5120   'ERASE ANY PRIOR INFO
5149 REM RESTORE CURSOR FOR USER RESPONSE
5150 LOCATE I,CP1
5160 NEXT I
5170 RETURN
```

Figure A.5: Display Dialog Subroutine

```
5400 REM          "INCH"
5401 ' ------------------------------
5402 '          INPUT CHARACTER
5403 '
5404 'CALLING PARAMETERS:
5405 '    NONE
5406 '
5407 'RETURNED PARAMETERS:
5408 '    CH$=INPUT CHARACTER
5409 '
5410 ' ------------------------------
5420 REM WAIT FOR INPUT CHARACTER
5430 CH$= INKEY$ : IF CH$="" THEN 5430
5440 Z=ASC(CH$)
5450 IF Z < 97 OR  Z > 122 THEN 5470
5460 Z=Z-32                          'CONVERT TO UPPER CASE
5470 CH$=CHR$(Z)
5480 RETURN
```

Figure A.6: Input Character Subroutine

```
5800 REM        "INDAT"
5801 ' ------------------------------
5802 '          INPUT DATA
5803 '
5804 'CALLING PARAMETERS:
5805 '    Q1$,Q2$= USER INSTRUCTIONS
5806 '    Q3$=NAME OF DATA ITEM
5807 '
5808 'RETURNED PARAMETERS:
5809 '    P$(K)=ARRAY OF DATA ITEMS
5810 '
5811 'COMMENT:ONE ITEM AT A TIME IS INPUT
5812 '          FIRST CALL IS WITH K=1
5813 '          K UPDATED AUTOMATICALLY
5814 '
5815 '-------------------------------
5820 GOSUB 5000                       'ASK QUESTIONS
5830 INPUT P$(K)                      'GET DATA
5840 REM ECHO QUESTION AND ANSWER
5850 LOCATE K+2,3
5860 PRINT Q3$;TAB(25);P$(K)
5870 K=K+1                            'UPDATE INDEX
5880 RETURN
```

Figure A.7: Input Data Subroutine

```
6200 REM           "INIT"
6201 ' -------------------------------
6202 '        INITIALIZE DISPLAY
6203 '
6204 'THIS ROUTINE CLEARS THE SCREEN
6205 '    AND PRINTS THE PROGRAM TITLE
6206 'CALLING PARAMETERS:
6207 '    N$=TITLE OF PROGRAM
6208 '
6209 'RETURNED PARAMETERS:
6210 '    NONE
6211 '
6212 ' -------------------------------
6220 CLS                               'CLEAR SCREEN
6230 PRINT N$    : PRINT               'TITLE
6240 KEY OFF
6250 RETURN
```

Figure A.8: Initialize Program and Display Subroutine

```
6600 REM           "INPAR"
6601 ' -------------------------------
6602 '        INPUT PARAMETERS
6603 '
6604 'CALLING PARAMETERS:
6605 '    Q1$,Q2$=USER INSTRUCTIONS
6606 '    Q3$=NAME OF DATA ITEM
6607 '
6608 'RETURNED PARAMETERS:
6609 '    PAR(K)=THE DATA ITEM OBTAINED
6610 '
6611 'COMMENT: CALL WITH K=1 FOR FIRST DATA ITEM
6612 '         K AUTOMATICALLY UPDATED
6613 '
6614 ' -------------------------------
6620 GOSUB 5000                        'ASK QUESTIONS
6630 INPUT PAR(K)                      'GET VALUE
6640 REM ECHO QUESTION AND ANSWER
6650 LOCATE K+2,3
6660 PRINT Q3$; TAB(24);
6670 PRINT USING "######,.##"; PAR(K)
6680 K=K+1
6690 RETURN
```

Figure A.9: Input Program Parameters Subroutine

```
7000 REM          "MENU"
7001 ' -------------------------------
7002 '          MENU PROGRAM
7003 '
7004 'THIS PROGRAM DISPLAYS A MENU
7005 '  AND CHOOSES A PROGRAM
7006 'CALLING PARAMETERS:
7007 '  N= NO. OF MENU ITEMS
7008 '  X$(I)= ARRAY OF PROGRAM NAMES
7009 '
7010 'RETURNED PARAMETERS:
7011 '  X=PROGRAM NUMBER CHOSEN
7012 '
7013 ' -------------------------------
7020 CLS
7030 FOR I= 1 TO N                   'DISPLAY MENU
7040   IF I=10 THEN PRINT 0; ELSE PRINT I;
7050    PRINT  "= " ; X$(I)
7060 NEXT I
7070 Q1$="" : Q2$=""
7080 Q3$="CHOOSE PROGRAM :"
7090 GOSUB 5000                      'ASK QUESTIONS
7100 GOSUB 5400                     'INPUT CHAR
7110 X= VAL(CH$)
7119 REM SEE IF CHAR IN RANGE
7120 IF X>=1 AND X<=N THEN RETURN
7130 IF X=0 AND N=10 THEN 7140 ELSE 7150
7140 X=10 : RETURN
7150 Q1$="ILLEGAL CHOICE, CHOOSE AGAIN"
7160 GOSUB 5000
7170 GOTO 7100
```

Figure A.10: Display Menu Subroutine

```
7400 REM            "PAUSE"
7401 ' --------------------------------
7402 '       WAIT FOR ANY KEY
7403 '
7404 'THIS ROUTINE WAITS FOR USER TO STRIKE KEY
7405 '
7406 'CALLING PARAMETERS:
7407 '  NONE
7408 '
7409 'RETURNED PARAMETERS
7410 '  NONE
7411 '
7412 ' --------------------------------
7420 Q1$="STRIKE ANY KEY TO CONTINUE"
7430 Q2$="" : Q3$=""
7440 GOSUB 5000                           'CALL DIALOG
7450 X$=INKEY$ : IF X$ = "" THEN 7450  'WAIT FOR KEY
7460 RETURN
```

Figure A.11: Pause Subroutine

```
7800 REM            "YESNO"
7801 ' --------------------------------
7802 '              YES-NO
7803 '
7804 'CALLING PARAMETERS:
7805 '  NONE
7806 '
7807 'RETURNED PARAMETERS:
7808 '  YN$= CONTAINS A Y OR N
7809 '
7810 ' --------------------------------
7820 REM WAIT FOR KEY TO BE STRUCK
7830 YN$=INKEY$ : IF YN$="" THEN 7830
7840 IF YN$="y" THEN YN$="Y"
7850 IF YN$="n" THEN YN$="N"
7860 IF YN$ = "Y" OR YN$ = "N" THEN 7890
7870 REM NOT YES OR NO TRY AGAIN
7880 GOTO 7830
7890 PRINT YN$  :  RETURN
```

Figure A.12: Yes or No Subroutine

□□□ APPENDIX B

HOW TO USE THE CENTRAL SUBROUTINES

Readers who would like to improve their programming skills should try writing their own programs. You can save a lot of time and effort by using the central subroutines in this book as part of your programs. This appendix will help you learn to use these central subroutines. We review here several of the subroutines and how they function. We also include sample programs that show how the subroutines can be used.

MENU SET-UP

The menu set-up subroutine begins at line 7000. This subroutine displays a menu on the screen and waits for the user to press a number key. The menu program then returns a value, which you use to select the program you want to run.

Figures B.1 and B.2 show the program listing and screen display for a sample menu selection. We set up the array X$(I) with the names of the available programs. We then set N = to the number of program choices and call the menu subroutine. The subroutine displays the names of the programs and waits for the user to make a selection. The subroutine then returns the value of the selected program. The returned value is used in an ON . . . GOSUB statement to select a program.

□□□

```
100 REM --------------------------------
110 N$=       "MENU DEMONSTRATION"
120 REM --------------------------------
130 GOSUB 6200                           'INITIALIZE
140 REM SET UP MENU ARRAY
150 X$(1)="PROGRAM 1"
160 X$(2)="PROGRAM 2"
170 X$(3)="PROGRAM 3"
180 X$(4)="PROGRAM 4"
190 N=4 : GOSUB 7000                     'DISPLAY MENU
200 ON X GOTO 210,220,230,240            'SELECT PROGRAM
210 PRINT X$(1); " CHOSEN" :END
220 PRINT X$(2); " CHOSEN" :END
230 PRINT X$(3); " CHOSEN" :END
240 PRINT X$(4); " CHOSEN" :END
```

Figure B.1: Program Listing: Sample Menu Selection

```
  1 = PROGRAM 1
  2 = PROGRAM 2
  3 = PROGRAM 3
  4 = PROGRAM 4









-----------------------------------------


CHOOSE PROGRAM :
```

Figure B.2: Screen Display: Sample Menu Selection

CHOOSING ANOTHER PROGRAM

All the programs in this book use the ANOTH subroutine. This subroutine asks the user whether he would like to run the program again. The subroutine displays three lines of data. The ANOTH subroutine generates the first and third data lines. You specify the second line when you call the subroutine.

The ANOTH routine returns a Y or an N in the variable YN$. The program tests this variable to decide whether it will run the program again.

Figures B.3 and B.4 show the program listing and a screen display for the ANOTH demonstration. Note that the sample program displays the question DEMONSTRATE THIS ROUTINE.

□□□

```
250 REM ----------------------------------------
260 N$= "DEMONSTRATION OF 'ANOTHER' SUBROUTINE"
270 REM ----------------------------------------
280 GOSUB 6200                           'INITIALIZE
290 Q2$="DEMONSTRATE THIS ROUTINE"
300 GOSUB 3400                           'ASK FOR ANOTHER
310 IF YN$="Y" THEN 250 ELSE END
```

Figure B.3: Program Listing: Demonstration of ANOTH Subroutine

```
DEMONSTRATION OF 'ANOTHER' SUBROUTINE









----------------------------------------
WOULD YOU LIKE TO
DEMONSTRATE THIS ROUTINE
AGAIN Y OR N ?
```

Figure B.4: Screen Display: Demonstration of ANOTH Subroutine

THE DIALOG SUBROUTINE

We use the DIALOG subroutine to display three lines of text at the bottom of the screen. You have the flexibility to generate three different questions; three questions or instructions will handle most programs you design. We often give an instruction on the first line, with questions on the second and third lines. This routine also draws a border and clears leftover text from previous questions. The routine exits with the cursor after the third question. Figures B.5 and B.6 show a program listing and screen display of a DIALOG demonstration.

□□□

```
320 REM ----------------------------------------
330 N$= "DEMONSTRATION OF 'DIALOG' SUBROUTINE"
340 REM ----------------------------------------
350 GOSUB 6200                       'INITIALIZE
360 REM SET UP QUESTIONS
370 Q1$="THIS IS FIRST QUESTION"
380 Q2$=""                           'A BLANK QUESTION
390 Q3$="THIS IS LAST QUESTION"
400 GOSUB 5000                       'SEND OUT THE QUESTIONS
410 END
```

Figure B.5: Program Listing: Demonstration of DIALOG Subroutine

```
----------------------------------------
THIS IS FIRST QUESTION

THIS IS LAST QUESTION
Ok
```

Figure B.6: Screen Display: Demonstration of DIALOG Subroutine

DATA INPUT SUBROUTINE

The INPAR program handles data input for many of the programs in this book and is easily used to create additional programs. You begin the data input process by clearing the screen with the INIT subroutine and setting the index K equal to 1. You are now ready to input program parameters. For each parameter, set Q3$ equal to the name of the parameter and call the subroutine at 6600. The INPAR subroutine asks the parameter name at the bottom of the screen and waits for input. The parameter then appears at the top of the screen. INPAR stores parameters in the array PAR(K) in the order of entry. Figures B.7 and B.8 show a program listing and screen display of the Data Input program.

□□□

```
420 REM -------------------------------
430 N$=    "DATA INPUT DEMONSTRATION"
440 REM -------------------------------
450 GOSUB 6200   : K=1                    'INITIALIZE
460 REM SET UP DIALOG AREA
470 Q1$="ENTER DATA" : Q2$=""
480 Q3$="RETAIL PRICE" : GOSUB 6600   'GET FIRST ITEM
490 Q3$="DISCOUNT (%)" : GOSUB 6600   'SECOND ITEM
500 PRINT : PRINT "PRICE = "; TAB(24)
510 PRINT USING "######,.##";PAR(1)-PAR(2)/100*PAR(1)
520 END
```

Figure B.7: Program Listing: Data Input Demonstration

```
DATA INPUT DEMONSTRATION

  RETAIL PRICE                 300.00
  DISCOUNT (%)                  10.00

PRICE =                        270.00
Ok









----------------------------------------
ENTER DATA

DISCOUNT (%)? 10
```

Figure B.8: Screen Display: Data Input Demonstration

□□□ APPENDIX C

USEFUL PRINTER SUBROUTINES

Your IBM printer outputs data in a number of interesting type styles. You can print in normal, expanded, condensed, emphasized, double-strike, and emphasized and double-strike modes. Figure C.1 shows the different printing modes.

You can use the subroutines in this appendix to gain access to your printer's different type styles. Emphasized mode is very useful for letter printing; condensed mode prints 132-column reports on 80-column paper.

Figure C.2 shows the menu selection program for printer control. Figure C.3 lists subroutines you can use to select the different type styles. Figure C.4 lists the program that uses the printer subroutines to produce the sample type styles in Figure C.1.

```
PRINTING MODES AVAILABLE ON IBM PRINTER

This is normal printing.

This is condensed printing.

This is expanded printing.

This is emphasized printing.

This is double-strike printing.

This is  emphasized and double-strike printing.
```

Figure C.1: Printing Modes Available on the IBM Printer

```
100 REM --------------------------------
110 N$=   "PRINTER CONTROL FUNCTIONS"
120 REM --------------------------------
130 GOSUB 6200
140 REM SET UP MENU ARRAY
150 X$(1)="CONDENSED MODE ON"
160 X$(2)="CONDENSED MODE OFF"
170 X$(3)="EXPANDED MODE ON"
180 X$(4)="EXPANDED MODE OFF"
190 X$(5)="EMPHASIZED MODE ON"
200 X$(6)="EMPHASIZED MODE OFF"
210 X$(7)="DOUBLE-STRIKE ON"
220 X$(8)="DOUBLE-STRIKE OFF"
230 X$(9)="PRINT SAMPLE TEXT"
240 N=9: GOSUB 7000                  'DISPLAY MENU
250 ON X GOSUB 270,320,370,420,470,520,570,620,670
260 GOTO 100
```

Figure C.2: Program Listing: Menu Selection for Printer Control

```
270 REM ------------------------------
280 N$=       "CONDENSED PRINT ON"
290 REM ------------------------------
300 LPRINT CHR$(15);
310 RETURN
320 REM ------------------------------
330 N$=      "CONDENSED PRINT OFF"
340 REM ------------------------------
350 LPRINT CHR$(18);
360 RETURN
370 REM ------------------------------
380 N$=       "EXPANDED PRINT ON"
390 REM ------------------------------
400 LPRINT CHR$(14);
410 RETURN
420 REM ------------------------------
430 N$=       "EXPANDED PRINT OFF"
440 REM ------------------------------
450 LPRINT CHR$(20);
460 RETURN
470 REM ------------------------------
480 N$=      "EMPHASIZED PRINT ON"
490 REM ------------------------------
500 LPRINT CHR$(27)+CHR$(69)
510 RETURN
520 REM ------------------------------
530 N$=      "EMPHASIZED PRINT OFF"
540 REM ------------------------------
550 LPRINT CHR$(27)+CHR$(70);
560 RETURN
570 REM ------------------------------
580 N$=        "DOUBLE-STRIKE ON"
590 REM ------------------------------
600 LPRINT CHR$(27)+CHR$(71);
610 RETURN
620 REM ------------------------------
630 N$=       "DOUBLE-STRIKE OFF"
640 REM ------------------------------
650 LPRINT CHR$(27)+CHR$(72);
660 RETURN
```

Figure C.3: Program Listing: Subroutines to Select Type Styles

```
670 REM ------------------------------
680 N$=          "SAMPLE TEXT"
690 REM ------------------------------
700 CLS
710 PRINT "TURN PRINTER ON, STRIKE ANY KEY WHEN READY"
720 GOSUB 5400                'WAIT FOR CHARACTER
730 GOSUB 470                 'USE EMPHASIZED PRINT IN TITLE
740 LPRINT
750 LPRINT "      PRINTING MODES AVAILABLE ON IBM PRINTER"
760 GOSUB 520
770 LPRINT  :  LPRINT  :  LPRINT
780 T1$="This is " : T2$="printing."
790 LPRINT T1$; "normal ";T2$ : LPRINT
800 GOSUB 270
810 LPRINT T1$; "condensed ";T2$ : LPRINT
820 GOSUB 320 : GOSUB 370
830 LPRINT T1$; "expanded ";T2$ : LPRINT
840 GOSUB 420 : GOSUB 470
850 LPRINT T1$; "emphasized ";T2$ : LPRINT
860 GOSUB 520 : GOSUB 570
870 LPRINT T1$; "double-strike ";T2$ : LPRINT
880 GOSUB 620
890 GOSUB 470 : GOSUB 570
900 LPRINT T1$; " emphasized and double-strike "; T2$
910 GOSUB 520 : GOSUB 620
920 END
```

Figure C.4: Program Listing:
Subroutines Used to Select Type Styles Shown in Figure C.1